UNDERSTANDING WEAPONS AND ARMS CONTROL

Titles of Related Interest

Related Journals*

*Sample copies available upon request

UNDERSTANDING WEAPONS AND ARMS CONTROL:
A GUIDE TO THE ISSUES

Fourth Edition, Revised

Teena Karsa Mayers

BRASSEY'S (US), Inc.
Maxwell Macmillan Pergamon Publishing Corp.

Washington · New York · London · Oxford
Beijing · Frankfurt · São Paulo · Sydney · Tokyo · Toronto

U.S.A. (Editorial)	Brassey's (US), Inc. 8000 Westpark Drive, 1st Floor, McLean, Virginia 22102, U.S.A.
(Orders)	Attn: Order Dept., Macmillan Publishing Co., Front & Brown Streets, Riverside, N.J. 08075
U.K. (Editorial)	Brassey's (UK) Ltd. 24 Gray's Inn Road, London WC1X 8HR, England
(Orders)	Brassey's (UK) Ltd. Headington Hill Hall, Oxford OX3 0BW, England
PEOPLE'S REPUBLIC **OF CHINA**	Pergamon Press, Room 4037, Quianmen Hotel, Beijing, People's Republic of China
FEDERAL REPUBLIC **OF GERMANY**	Pergamon Press GmbH, Hammerweg 6, D-6242 Kronberg, Federal Republic of Germany
BRAZIL	Pergamon Editora Ltda, Rua Eça de Queiros, 346, CEP 04011, Paraiso, Sao Paulo, Brazil
AUSTRALIA	Brassey's Australia, P.O. Box 544, Potts Point, N.S.W. 2011, Australia
JAPAN	Pergamon Press, 5th Floor, Matsuoka Central Building, 1-7-1 Nishishinjuku, Shinjuku-ku, Tokyo 160, Japan
CANADA	Pergamon Press Canada, Suite No. 271, 253 College Street, Toronto, Ontario, Canada M5T 1R5

Copyright © 1991 Brassey's (US), Inc.

*Brassey's (US), Inc., books are available at special discounts for bulk
purchases for sales promotions, premiums, fund-raising, or educational use
through the Special Sales Director, Macmillan Publishing Company,
866 Third Avenue, New York, NY 10022.*

Library of Congress Cataloging-in-Publication Data

Mayers, Teena.
  Understanding weapons and arms control: a guide to the issues/
Teena Karsa Mayers.—4th ed., rev.
    p. cm.
  Rev. ed. of: Understanding nuclear weapons and arms control. 3rd
ed., rev. 1986.
  Includes bibliographical references.
  ISBN 0-08-037438-7
  1. Nuclear arms control—Popular works. 2. Nuclear weapons—
—Popular works. 3. Arms control—Popular works. 4. Munitions—
—Popular works. I. Mayers, Teena. Understanding nuclear weapons
and arms control. II. Title.
JX1974.7.M36   1990
327.1'74—dc20   90-1834
                                                             CIP
                                                             Rev.

British Library Cataloguing in Publication Data

Mayers, Teena Karsa
  Understanding weapons and arms control.—4th ed. rev.
  1. Arms control
  I. Title II. Mayers, Teena Karsa. Understanding nuclear
  weapons and arms control
  327.174

  ISBN 0-08-037438-7

Printed in the United States of America

Contents

Introduction

Because the arms control issue is so vital to our national security, Teena Mayers, the author, devised this book as a guide to understanding a complicated topic. This book provides a brief history of the nuclear arms race; facts on the basics of arms control; the current status of negotiations between the United States and the Soviet Union; international concerns; conventional forces; chemical and biological weapons, and the authority to release nuclear weapons; existing treaties and agreements; and the effects of nuclear war.

Formerly an Administrator of Special Projects with the U.S. Arms Control and Disarmament Agency, Teena Mayers participated in preliminary meetings and discussions for plenary sessions with the Soviet Union as a member of the Advisors and Experts Group on the SALT II Delegation in Geneva; restructured and edited the 500-page SALT II negotiating history of the Treaty and Protocol covering seven years of negotiations; and served as one of the principals of the Public Affairs SALT Task Force. She designed and edited the agency's 1980 Annual Report and performed an in-depth statistical analysis for the United Nations on the "Economic and Social Consequences of the Arms Race and Military Expenditures" with comparative statistics on defense, health, housing, education, and research development.

Simple in style, content, and format, the facts and information in this guide were assembled from documents published by the United States government and other materials in the public domain.

Specialists in arms control and U.S.-Soviet affairs have reviewed and approved the text:

The Honorable Paul C. Warnke, former Assistant Secretary of Defense for International Security Affairs, U.S. Chief SALT II Negotiator, and Director of the U.S. Arms Control and Disarmament Agency.

Major General John Ralph, former Commandant of the Industrial College of the Armed Forces, Executive Secretary to the SALT Delegation in Geneva, and Senior Military Advisor to the U.S. Arms Control and Disarmament Agency.

Vice Admiral John Marshall Lee, USN (Ret.), former Vice Director, NATO Military Staff; Commander, 7th Fleet Amphibious Forces, Western Pacific; and Assistant Director of the U.S. Arms Control and Disarmament Agency.

Acknowledgments:

Robert S. Norris, Senior Analyst
Natural Resources Defense Council;

Michael Krepon, Senior Fellow
Carnegie Endowment for International Peace; and

Robert Guldin, Associate Editor
Arms Control Association.

UNDERSTANDING WEAPONS AND ARMS CONTROL

Section I

1

Since the dawn of the nuclear age, debate has raged about the military uses of nuclear weapons and the strategic nuclear policy that the United States should follow.

The strategic superiority that would enable either side to prevail in a nuclear war will not be gained at the bargaining table. There is nothing to indicate that it can be gained in an arms race.

The best that can be hoped for is a stable strategic balance that can be maintained at lower levels, and for this, no administration has found an answer that does not require negotiated arms control.

1945 · 1952   The Truman Years

"... the atomic bomb is a means of destruction
hitherto unknown, against which there can be
no adequate military defense, and in the
employment of which no single nation can in
fact have a monopoly."

Harry S. Truman
November 15, 1945

When President Truman authorized the use of two atomic bombs in 1945 against the Japanese cities of Hiroshima and Nagasaki, the nature of international security was changed drastically and irrevocably.

In the late 1940s, following the conclusion of World War II, the wartime alliance between the United States and the Soviet Union deteriorated. The spoils of war resulted in the Soviet establishment of puppet regimes in Eastern European countries and the creation of East Germany as an additional satellite. Anti-communist sentiments grew in the United States when it became more and more obvious that the Soviet Union constituted a major threat to world stability.

Even though the United States had a monopoly of **atomic bombs** in the years 1945–1949, some officials and scientists argued that atomic weapons should not be considered as merely another type of military weapon, and that measures should be taken to prevent their use ever again. In their view, atomic weapons could not be used for warfare because of their enormous destructive power.

atomic bombs

Others contended that the U.S. technological lead should and could be exploited. During the Truman administration, these differing views came into sharp conflict over the development of the **hydrogen** or **thermonuclear bomb**, immensely more powerful than the original atomic bomb.

hydrogen or thermonuclear bomb

3

Although President Truman approved the development of the hydrogen bomb, he also sought unsuccessfully to control nuclear weapons. For example, the **Baruch Plan** was proposed to the United Nations in 1946. This plan called for an international agency to ensure that atomic energy would be used solely for peaceful purposes. The Soviets, however, insisted that U.S. nuclear weapons be destroyed before an international control agency was established. The United States insisted that the international agency be established before it would relinquish sole possession of the bomb. The two countries were unable to compromise the two positions.

Baruch Plan

When the Soviet Union detonated its first atomic weapon in 1949, the international situation worsened. And the beginning of the Korean War in 1950 effectively precluded possibilities of U.S.-Soviet agreement on control of atomic weaponry.

Soon thereafter, intelligence reports revealed that the Soviets were actively at work on the development of the hydrogen bomb. President Truman felt that he had no alternative but to take the next major step in the arms race. In 1952, the United States successfully tested a thermonuclear, or hydrogen, bomb. A year later the Soviet Union matched this feat.

The nuclear race was on. . . .

1953 · 1960 The Eisenhower Years

". . . we witness today, in the power of nuclear weapons, a new and deadly dimension to the ancient horror of war. Humanity has now achieved, for the first time in its history, the power to end its history."

Dwight D. Eisenhower
September 19, 1956

During the Eisenhower administration, a state of political tension and military rivalry between the United States and the Soviet Union, known as the **Cold War,** doomed any hopes of arms control. Proposals and counterproposals were made but failed to bring to fruition any control or limitation of nuclear weapons.

Cold War

Moreover, the Eisenhower administration relied heavily on nuclear weapons as a substitute for improved conventional forces—soldiers, tanks, and aircraft—which were far more costly.

John Foster Dulles, Eisenhower's Secretary of State, announced a policy of **massive retaliation**—a doctrine whereby the United States might respond with nuclear weapons to any Soviet challenge any place in the world. President Eisenhower's Secretary of Defense, Charles Wilson, referred to this as "more bang for the buck." The vacillation of the Truman administration between disarmament and a nuclear buildup was soon resolved by Eisenhower's strong stand for **nuclear superiority.**

massive retaliation

nuclear superiority

Despite the huge American lead in nuclear weapons that existed in the 1950s, the doctrine of "massive retaliation" achieved little success. United States' superiority did not prevent the Soviets from suppressing the Hungarian Freedom Fighters in the 1956 uprising, nor did it help liberate other captive peoples of Eastern Europe.

During these years, however, thousands of so-called *tactical nuclear weapons*—artillery shells, bombs, and short-range missiles with nuclear warheads—were developed and deployed in Central Europe for use in a ground campaign by land armies. Their purpose was to deter and, if necessary, defend U.S. and NATO forces against a Soviet and Warsaw Pact conventional attack. These "tactical nuclear weapons" were considered essential to give the United States and its NATO allies a meaningful edge against the superior numbers of Soviet conventional forces.

When the Korean War ended early in President Eisenhower's administration, there were reports that threats by the administration to use nuclear weapons had played a key part in achieving the armistice. Others believed Joseph Stalin's death in 1953 was the critical turning point.

Notwithstanding his announced policy of "nuclear superiority," Eisenhower made several attempts at arms limitations and even appointed a cabinet-level arms control advisor in 1955.

In 1957, the nation was shocked when the Soviets launched the Sputnik satellite—the first to orbit the globe. More ominous was the fact that the Soviets had successfully tested an *intercontinental ballistic missile (ICBM).* Then came the *Gaither Report,* a study

authorized by President Eisenhower called "Deterrence and Survival in the Nuclear Age," which concluded that the Soviet Union would soon achieve an ICBM force of sufficient numbers to launch a surprise attack against the United States. The fear that the Soviets were developing ICBM superiority was expressed as the *missile gap.*

Under Eisenhower, the United States increased its bomber force and built intercontinental ballistic missiles (ICBMs). By the end of his term, the United States had about 6200 nuclear weapons. The Soviets, who in 1952 had no intercontinental bombers, no submarine-launched missiles, and no intercontinental ballistic missiles, had developed bombers and ICBMs by 1960—but only a fraction of the numbers in the U.S. arsenal.

Although negotiations began in 1958 to ban nuclear testing, when he left office in 1960, Eisenhower was vocally disappointed by the lack of progress in arms control.

The nuclear race continued. . . .

1962

". . . the survivors would envy the dead."
Nikita Khrushchev

1961 · 1968   The Kennedy-Johnson Years

*". . . A nuclear disaster, spread by winds and
waters and fear, could well engulf the great and
the small, the rich and the poor, the committed
and uncommitted alike. Mankind must put an
end to war or war will put an end to mankind."*

John F. Kennedy
September 25, 1961

*". . . I want to be the President who helped to
end hatred among his fellow men and who
promoted love among the people of all races and
all religions and all parties. I want to be the
President who helped to end war among the
brothers of this earth."*

Lyndon B. Johnson
March 15, 1965

President Kennedy came to office after a 1960
campaign in which he had warned of a "missile gap"
whereby the Soviets had achieved or were achieving
a significant advantage in strategic nuclear weapons.
When the United States started to receive the first
pictures from space, it became clear that the real gap
favored the United States by a wide margin.

In the beginning of the Kennedy administration,
U.S.-Soviet tensions were running high. Kennedy and
his defense officials felt that the Eisenhower-Dulles
strategy of "massive retaliation" made little sense and
did not take account of the rapidly growing Soviet
nuclear arsenal. Conventional weapons would also
have to play an important role. Kennedy therefore
authorized a buildup of both nuclear and conventional
forces.

flexible
response

President Kennedy's buildup, however, was based on a different philosophy from Eisenhower's. The overall military doctrine during the Kennedy-Johnson years changed from "massive retaliation" to what became known as *flexible response*. The idea was to acquire the military forces that could deal flexibly with varying levels of Soviet aggression.

Under the direction of Secretary of Defense Robert McNamara, conventional forces were improved as the primary defense against conventional attack. The first-use of nuclear weapons was not ruled out, but any such use would occur only after Western forces had attempted a conventional battlefield defense but were being overwhelmed by Soviet forces. In such an event, the President would authorize the use of NATO's tactical battlefield nuclear weapons. Escalation to long-range strategic nuclear attacks on Soviet territory was contemplated only as a last resort to avoid total defeat.

triad

The strategic weapons programs initiated at the start of the Kennedy administration led to the formation of our present *triad* of strategic nuclear weapons: *intercontinental ballistic missiles (ICBMs), strategic bombers,* and *submarine-launched ballistic missiles*

SLBMs
(SLBMs).

Unlike missile silos or bomber bases on land, which could be located and targeted by the Soviets, submarines at sea—the third leg of the triad—were virtually invulnerable. When the first Polaris missile submarine went to sea, the United States was guaranteed a "second strike" capability; i.e., if our ground-based missiles and bombers were destroyed by a Soviet attack, our missile submarines could then respond with a retaliatory strike that would inflict unacceptable damage on the Soviet Union. For this purpose, Secretary McNamara calculated that 1000 land-based missiles and 41 submarines would be more than adequate. Although we have approximately the same number of strategic nuclear delivery vehicles today, the total number of warheads at that time was only a fraction of those in the current United States' force.

Strategies other than "flexible response" were also being considered such as **controlled response,** also known as **counterforce**, emphasizing the targeting of Soviet nuclear forces rather than cities, as contemplated by Eisenhower's doctrine of "massive retaliation." But Secretary McNamara concluded that the only realistic strategic nuclear strategy was that of **deterrence by assured retaliatory capability**. Since neither side possessed the means to defend itself against nuclear attack, the best way to deter the adversary was to have the ability to retaliate with unacceptable consequences in the event of an attack. In popular terms this strategy became known as **mutual assured destruction (MAD)**.

controlled response

counterforce

deterrence by assured retaliatory capability

mutual assured destruction (MAD)

When Lyndon Johnson was elected President in 1964, McNamara had established "deterrence" as the central role of U.S. nuclear forces. Under the policy of deterrence, the purpose of nuclear weapons is to prevent a potential adversary from using or threatening to use its nuclear weapons against the United States or its allies.

The most serious confrontation between the United States and the Soviet Union occurred when Soviet leader Khrushchev attempted to place intermediate-range missiles in Cuba. President Kennedy responded by imposing a "quarantine" or blockade of naval ships around Cuba that resulted in the withdrawal of the Soviet nuclear missiles. Some Soviet face-saving was afforded by President Kennedy's decision to dismantle U.S. missiles based in Turkey. Some analysts of the **Cuban Missile Crisis** argue that the successful outcome was due to U.S. strategic nuclear superiority, which, in their opinion, had proved that strategic superiority offered important political advantages. Other strategists, including key U.S. participants in the Cuban Missile Crisis, rejected these claims. They felt that U.S. advantage in conventional forces around

Cuban Missile Crisis

Cuba, especially our clear naval superiority, was responsible for the favorable outcome. The parties appear to have recognized that an attempt to resolve the dispute with nuclear weapons would mean unacceptable damage to both countries.

The Kennedy-Johnson years saw the first major successes in nuclear arms control. The **Limited Test Ban Treaty (LTBT)**, putting an end to atmospheric tests of nuclear weapons, was completed in 1963. In the same year, the Soviet Union and the United States established the **hotline** teletype to enable leaders of both countries to communicate at a time of crisis.

Limited Test Ban Treaty

hotline

In 1967, the **Outer Space Treaty,** banning the deployment of nuclear weapons in outer space, was completed and signed by the United States and the Soviet Union. In 1968, agreement was reached on the **NonProliferation Treaty (NPT)** directed against the acquisition of nuclear weapons by additional countries.

Outer Space Treaty

NPT

In the last two years of Lyndon Johnson's presidency, efforts were made to initiate talks on limiting strategic nuclear arms. Both sides agreed privately that the first **Strategic Arms Limitation Talks (SALT)** would begin in the fall of 1968. But on that day in August 1968 when these talks were to be announced, Soviet forces moved into Czechoslovakia to head off the growing unrest in that country. This, followed by the presidential election and a change of administration, delayed the actual start of the talks for a year.

SALT

During this time, the deployment of U.S. missiles with a new technological development called **multiple independently-targetable reentry vehicles (MIRVs)**—a single missile carrying multiple warheads that separate in outer space to strike targets hundreds of miles from each other—made control of nuclear weapons more difficult and less effective.

MIRVs

The nuclear race accelerated. . . .

1969 · 1976   The Nixon-Ford Years

*". . . potential enemies must know that we will
respond to whatever degree is required to protect
our interests. They must also know that they
will only worsen their situation by escalating the
level of violence."*

Richard Nixon
February 25, 1971

*". . . the weapons we hold today, and those
we plan for the future, give America a mighty
power. But with such power comes a mighty
responsibility. We must never forget the purpose
for which our arsenal is intended. That purpose
is not to terrify the weak, to provoke armed
confrontation, nor lay claim to that which is
not ours . . ."*

Gerald Ford
May 10, 1976

Like the Presidents who immediately preceded him,
Richard Nixon campaigned for the U.S. presidency in
1968 on a platform that called for regaining American
nuclear superiority. Early in his administration, however, he became the first president to accept the goal
of "sufficiency." He recognized that it was impossible
to regain a position where the United States would
threaten Soviet destruction without concern about the
consequences to the United States.

Soviet ICBMs had increased from 20 when President
Kennedy took office, to 200 when President Johnson
was elected, and to 800 in 1969. No matter how many
additional nuclear missiles the United States might
acquire, the Soviet forces had grown so large that a
nuclear exchange would devastate both countries.

parity

To counter the growing numbers of Soviet ICBMs, the United States responded with MIRVs. This made possible a several-fold increase in the number of warheads that could be aimed at Soviet targets. By the mid-1970s the Soviets also achieved this MIRV technology, resulting in a large increase in the Soviet warhead arsenal. Under these circumstances, President Nixon and his principal international security advisor, Henry Kissinger, recognized that "nuclear superiority" was no longer possible and that a condition of rough **parity** was inevitable.

detente

The rejection of "superiority" as a goal and the acceptance of "parity" made negotiations possible. The Nixon-Kissinger concept of **detente**—a lessening of tensions—was that relations could be improved by involving the Soviets in a pattern of cooperative relationships such as trade and cultural exchanges, as well as arms control. If "detente" could make the Soviets an involved participant in international economic life, it was hoped that Soviet adventurism would be checked. The continuing rivalry and intermittent animosity between the two countries led some to reject the concept of "detente." This disillusionment probably reflected exaggerated hopes. "Detente" is not, it must be remembered, anything more than a moderation of rivalry. It is not a synonym for friendship.

SALT I

ABM Treaty

Although the Nixon administration took steps leading to a large strategic buildup, it also took several important arms control initiatives. By May 1972, two agreements were signed. The first severely limited development and deployment of **defensive** anti-ballistic missiles (ABMs)—missiles designed to destroy attacking missiles enroute to their targets. The **ABM Treaty** provided initially that each side could deploy "defensive missile systems" at no more than two sites. A 1974 agreement reduced the permitted number to one site for each country.

By signing the ABM Treaty, both countries recognized that current and future technology could not provide an adequate and effective defense against nuclear attack. Continuing to build ABM systems would only stimulate the acquisition of even more warheads to overwhelm that defense.

The other part of what came to be called SALT I was an **Interim Agreement on Offensive Weapons** that essentially froze the number of launchers of ballistic missiles. Neither the United States nor the Soviet Union could add to its number of ICBM underground silos in existence or under construction. New missile-carrying submarines could be built, but this would require compensating reductions in the number of ICBM silos. Since the Interim Agreement on *offensive* arms limitations was not a treaty requiring approval of two-thirds of the Senate, it was sent to both Houses of Congress as an Executive Agreement to last for five years or until replaced by a longer-term treaty. Both accords—the ABM Treaty and the Interim Agreement—were overwhelmingly approved. *Interim Agreement*

Despite difficulties with detente, the SALT talks continued, and the Nixon-Ford years witnessed real progress toward conclusion of a SALT II agreement. In these arms control negotiations, both sides were working under the assumption that a strategic nuclear exchange would mean "mutual assured destruction."

There was also real progress in the technology of nuclear weapons. The Soviet Union began to deploy a new generation of land-based missiles, SS-17s, SS-18s, and SS-19s, far superior to their predecessors—the SS-9s and SS-11s—that could threaten U.S. land-based missiles. As a result, in 1974, Secretary of Defense James Schlesinger proposed greater emphasis on **counterforce capability**—whereby American missiles would be developed, deployed, and targeted to carry out "selective strikes" against Soviet military targets. This element of nuclear strategy was previously given secondary importance by Secretary of Defense McNamara during the Kennedy and Johnson administrations. *counterforce capability*

As long as both sides were willing to operate under the principle that nuclear war could be averted if both sides had an assured ability to retaliate, the need *war-fighting strategy* for new offensive weapons would be limited and the strategic balance would remain stable. But this new "counterforce" policy appeared to contemplate the need for a force that could conduct a "selective and sophisicated" nuclear war. Schlesinger conjectured that Soviet capabilities were beginning to fit a nuclear **war-fighting strategy**, and that preservation of deterrence required new U.S. counterforce weapons. Accordingly, he authorized further development of the **experimental missile (MX),** which would have 10 warheads of unparalleled accuracy.

Shortly after he succeeded Richard Nixon, Gerald Ford met in November 1974 with General Secretary Leonid Brezhnev in the Soviet port of **Vladivostok.** Important concessions made there were expected to make possible the speedy completion of a SALT II treaty controlling strategic offensive weapons.

Before the Vladivostok meeting, the Soviets pressed for higher numbers of launchers to compensate for the British, French, and Chinese nuclear arsenals targeted against the Soviet Union. In addition, the Soviet negotiators had insisted that the treaty include the U.S. nuclear warheads on aircraft based in Europe and on naval aircraft carriers adjacent to Soviet territory. Because of the complications with U.S. allies that the latter would present, the United States refused to accept these proposals and insisted on deferring these positions for further negotiation after a SALT II agreement had been signed. The U.S. considered the Soviet demand for numerical advantage to be unacceptable, at least on political grounds. The United States also insisted on including the Soviet Backfire bomber, of shorter range than U.S. strategic bombers but considered capable of reaching some U.S. targets. The Soviets refused to budge, and negotiations on the Backfire were also deferred.

At Vladivostok, Mr. Brezhnev accepted 1) the principle of equal ceilings of strategic weapons launchers; 2) deferral of the issue of American forward-based systems—weapons based on the periphery of the Soviet

16

Union—and 3) deferral of the issue of the Backfire bomber.

Completion of a SALT II treaty in either 1975 or 1976 was, however, prevented by two factors. The first was the lack of agreement on the treatment of **cruise missiles**—pilotless aircraft capable of incomparable accuracy. The Vladivostok understanding included ceilings on ASBMs—air-to-surface ballistic missiles launched from an airplane and capable of reaching targets thousands of miles away—a system that has never been deployed. But the United States maintained that cruise missiles were not subject to the same ceilings.

cruise missiles

The second factor, and probably the more important, was the American political situation. Before these issues were cleared up, President Ford found himself involved in a close contest with California Governor Ronald Reagan for the 1976 presidential nomination and was concerned that the SALT process would become a political issue. In an important segment of the American public, there was growing resistance to negotiating with the Russians and to the SALT process.

The arms control talks were stalled. . . .

1978

". . . as for the Soviet Union, it considers that approximate equilibrium and parity are enough for defense needs. We do not set ourselves the goal of gaining military superiority. We also know that this very concept loses its meaning with the present enormous stockpiles of nuclear weapons and systems for their delivery. . ."

Leonid I. Brezhnev

1977 · 1980   The Carter Years

". . . the level of nuclear armaments could grow
by tens of thousands, and the same situation
could well occur with advanced conventional
weapons. The temptation to use these weapons,
for fear that someone else might do it first,
would be almost irresistible."

Jimmy Carter
October 4, 1977

President Jimmy Carter took office with an elo-
quent call for reduction and eventual elimination of
nuclear weapons. He pledged to cut back defense spend-
ing on an annual basis by $5 billion to $7 billion.

In the last days of the Ford administration, a
U.S. official intelligence-gathering analysis concluded
that the aim of the Soviet Union was to gain military
superiority over the United States, that its strategic
doctrine contemplated that a nuclear war could be
fought and won, and that the Soviets were substantially
outspending the United States on defense.

Reports from this analysis soon affected the defense
debate in the early days of President Carter's term.
After initially cutting defense funds, President Carter
subsequently raised them more than enough to cover
the effects of inflation.

Instead of seeking rapid completion of a SALT II *comprehensive*
Treaty along the lines that had been negotiated since *package*
Vladivostok, President Carter presented the Russians in
March 1977 with what was called a **comprehensive
package.** The U.S. proposal called for deep cuts in
levels substantially below the Vladivostok ceilings.
Specifically, it called for a 50 percent reduction in
the Soviets' large land-based missiles, the SS-18s, but
no deep cuts in those systems where the United States
had the advantage, such as strategic bombers and

19

submarine missiles with multiple warheads. However, in return, the United States offered to stop development of the MX missile. The Soviet leadership rejected both this "comprehensive package" and a proposed alternative. The alternative was to sign a treaty based on the Vladivostok understanding without agreeing to controls over American cruise missiles or the Soviet Backfire bomber.

SALT II Treaty

After a short delay, however, negotiations recommenced in Geneva in May 1977. Notwithstanding the growing tension and mistrust in superpower relations, the negotiations continued and the **SALT II Treaty** was finally signed in June 1979. SALT II contained many elements of the comprehensive package but not at levels as low as the first Carter proposal and without reductions in the Soviet SS-18 missiles.

Comprehensive Test Ban (CTB)

A series of other arms control initiatives were also undertaken. Most important was the negotiation of a **Comprehensive Test Ban (CTB)** on any further testing of nuclear explosive devices. The British joined the Soviets and Americans in these talks on a CTB.

ratification

Opposition to the SALT II Treaty had been growing in the U.S. Senate for months. The Treaty did not require cuts in operational bombers and submarine MIRVed missiles where the U.S. was superior, but some senators were concerned because the SALT II agreement did not count Soviet Backfire bombers, allowed only the Soviets to have missiles as large as the SS-18s, and permitted the Soviets to retain a much larger land-based missile force that the United States. **Ratification** of a treaty requires a two-thirds' vote of approval in the Senate. To acquire the necessary support, the Carter administration mounted a concerted campaign. Secretary of Defense Harold Brown announced the decision to go ahead with the large MX missile and its complicated race-track system of deployment and a commitment to a larger defense buildup. A majority of the Senate Foreign Relations Committee recommended ratification of Salt II, but by a narrow margin.

Then, in the summer of 1979, U.S. intelligence photos from a satellite revealed a Soviet military brigade on maneuvers in Cuba. Recalling the Cuban Missile Crisis of 1962, opponents of SALT viewed this with alarm as another act of Soviet provocation. Further investigation revealed that the Soviet brigade of less than 3000 had been in Cuba for years.

In September 1979, Vice President Walter Mondale, on a visit to China, indicated United States willingness to sell the Chinese military-related equipment. At this same time, there were reports that the United States was moving ahead with plans to install nuclear missiles in Europe capable of striking targets in the Soviet Union.

On December 24, 1979, the Soviet Union launched a massive invasion of Afghanistan.

U.S.-Soviet relations plummeted to the lowest level since the Stalin era. President Carter ordered that SALT II be placed on "hold" with no further attempt to gain ratification. The United States cut off most of its grain shipments and all of its technology from Soviet trade. Cultural and scientific exchanges were ended. U.S.-Soviet relations were placed in deep freeze.

In the Carter years, opponents of the strategic nuclear policy based on the "mutual assured destruction" doctrine of deterrence continued to exert substantial influence. As a consequence, President Carter authorized changes in U.S. strategy for using nuclear weapons in the event of war. **Presidential Directive 59** set forth a strategy of selective and flexible use of nuclear weapons based on the assumption that the Soviets might start a "limited nuclear war." It called for the United States to be prepared to respond with "selective strikes" against various categories of Soviet military and industrial targets over a protracted period of time.

Presidential Directive 59

Critics assailed the new strategy as one based on a theory that a nuclear war could be limited and could be fought by the United States to a successful conclusion. U.S. officials, particularly Secretary of Defense Harold Brown, sought to rationalize the directive (PD 59) as **not** being a departure from the "deterrence" strategy. Instead, they argued, it was to be viewed simply as a precautionary measure—the U.S. must be prepared to deny the Soviets any advantage, whatever level of attack they might elect to conduct. U.S. forces could and should be designed to disabuse them of notions of victory.

Many advocates of arms control found these nuclear war-fighting concepts—such as those represented in PD 59—to be incompatible with arms control as they increased requirements for nuclear forces and increasingly threatened the security of both sides.

shell game President Carter then announced his decision to go ahead with the deployment of 200 MX missiles and a complicated **shell game** method—a multiple-based **race-track** system of deployment. Two hundred missiles would have moved among 4600 shelters in an effort to confuse Soviet military planners.

Euromissiles The Carter administration also authorized, and NATO approved in late 1979, the deployment of two new missiles in Europe that could reach targets in the Soviet Union. These missiles, the **Pershing II** and the ground-launched **cruise missile,** were intended as a response to a Soviet buildup of SS-20 missiles—an intermediate-range missile targeted mostly at Europe. A Western response was regarded as politically imperative. The NATO two-track response included preparation for deployment of 572 Pershing IIs and ground-launched cruise missiles, unless an arms control agreement made such deployments unnecessary. If the negotiations were unsuccessful, ground-launched cruise missiles would be placed in five NATO countries. The Federal Republic of Germany would receive both ground-launched cruise missiles and the Pershing IIs—a ballistic missile that could strike Soviet targets (but probably not Moscow) in six to eight minutes.

The arms control agreements were suspended. . . .

1981 · 1988 The Reagan Years

". . . we must seek agreements which are verifiable, equitable, and militarily significant. Agreements that provide only the appearance of arms control breed dangerous illusions."

Ronald Reagan
May 9, 1982

During his presidential campaign, President Reagan had suggested that arms control could be facilitated by negotiating from a position of strength. He argued that the United States had fallen behind, and therefore the priority task was to build up our strategic nuclear forces to regain a **margin of safety.** He proposed a $180 billion five-year strategic modernization program which would add 7000 new weapons to the U.S. stockpile over ten years.

margin of safety

He pledged to deploy the MX missile but cut back Carter's original planned force from 200 to 100 missiles and rejected Carter's shell-game, race-track basing mode. Claiming it was too vulnerable and not cost-effective, President Reagan proposed a **dense-pack** basing mode where 100 MX missiles would be spaced 1800 feet apart in hardened silos in a 14-mile-long rectangle. Supposedly, the missiles would survive since an attack could not be timed precisely enough to strike all silos at the same time, and the explosion of the first warheads to arrive would create conditions that would disable the later arrivals—an effect called **"fratricide."**

fratricide

Congress would not support this basing plan, stating that it was even less survivable than the Carter race-track proposal. President Reagan then, in 1983, appointed a panel entitled the President's Commission on Strategic Forces to review MX alternatives. This panel became known as the Scowcroft Commission.

Some Reagan administration officials talked about the possibility of limited nuclear war. The McNamara doctrine that nuclear forces could serve only as a "deterrent" to nuclear attack was criticized as inaccurate. In the early Reagan years, Defense Department documents expanded the "minimum purposes" of these forces to include the ability to "prevail" and end a nuclear war on terms favorable to the United States.

The SALT II Treaty remained unratified and the Comprehensive Test Ban negotiations were suspended. The new administration displayed no sense of urgency about resuming talks with the Soviets on control of nuclear weapons.

But President Reagan was faced with a vocal and growing anti-nuclear movement in Europe and the "Freeze" campaign in the United States calling for an end to production and testing of nuclear weapons.

The Soviet Union was replacing its SS-4s and SS-5s with a new mobile missile, the SS-20, which had three accurate warheads each that could reach all of Europe as well as Asian targets when stationed east of the Ural Mountains.

dual-track decision Because of the threat of this new missile and the perception that the Soviet conventional forces were superior, NATO, in 1979, decided to modernize its theater nuclear forces with the deployment in Europe of 464 ground-launched cruise missiles and 108 Pershing II ballistic missiles beginning in 1983. This was known as the ***dual-track decision*** because it contemplated concurrent efforts to obtain an arms control agreement with the Soviet Union to limit its long-range theater nuclear forces, primarily the SS-20s.

INF Talks In response to pressures from Western Europeans— who had become troubled by official American statements about limited nuclear war, the scheduled deployment of the Pershings and cruise missiles, and the Reagan administration's hardline rhetoric—negotiations on ***Intermediate-range Nuclear Forces (INF)*** began in Geneva on November 30, 1981.

The Soviet objective in the talks was to block the deployment of the Pershing IIs and cruise missiles in Europe carrying a total of 572 warheads. The Reagan administration's opening negotiating position was that these missiles would be deployed unless the Soviet Union agreed to eliminate all of its intermediate-range ballistic missiles—the SS-20s with three warheads each, and older SS-4s and SS-5s with single warheads—a total of approximately 600 missiles with about 1200 warheads targeted against Western Europe. This Reagan position became known as the **zero-option.** *zero-option*

Both sides subsequently modified their positions. The U.S.S.R. first proposed withdrawing a substantial number of SS-20s from European Russia, remaining free to redeploy them against China and U.S. bases in South Korea and Japan. Eventually, the Soviet position was clarified to provide for destruction of some SS-20s as well as the remaining SS-4s and SS-5s together with a freeze on SS-20s aimed at Asian targets. The Soviets argued that this would eliminate more warheads than the 572 involved in the planned NATO deployment. They also contended that this would do no more than balance the intermediate-range missiles directed at the Soviet Union by NATO, including the British and French.

This reduction was not deep enough to satisfy NATO. Although NATO agreed to lower its deployment of Pershing IIs and cruise missiles in return for Soviet SS-20 cuts, this option was not satisfactory to the Kremlin, which insisted on no new missile deployments by NATO.

In July 1982, secret discussions were taking place informally between Ambassadors Paul Nitze and Yuli Kvitsinsky on the major issues in the negotiations. The proposal resulting from their discussions later became known as the **walk in the woods** formula. This formula suggested that the United States might be prepared to forego deployment of the Pershing II missiles but would proceed with 300 cruise missiles with 300 warheads in exchange for Soviet reductions to 75 SS-20s with 225 warheads. The United States government rejected the *"walk in the woods"* formula, arguing that both systems were necessary to offset the Soviet advantage in this area. The Soviet Union then announced its rejection.

By winter of 1983, the talks had reached an impasse. When the deployment of the American missiles began in December 1983, the Soviets walked out of the talks.

The talks resumed in January 1985. Intermediate-range nuclear force reductions were made the subject of one of the three concurrent negotiations, the others being on space-based systems (SDI and ASAT) and strategic range systems.

The negotiations on intermediate nuclear forces (INF) were especially difficult because many countries in the European theater had varying interests and perceptions of the problems involved. However, the accession of Mikhail Gorbachev to the Soviet leadership in March 1985 gave the talks greater impetus. In late 1985, President Reagan and the new Soviet leader met in Geneva for the first of their four summits.

In January 1986, General Secretary Gorbachev issued a statement calling for the elimination of all nuclear weapons by the year 2000. He proposed to eliminate all Soviet SS-20s in return for the elimination of the American Pershing II ballistic missiles and ground-launched cruise missiles stationed in the United Kingdom, Germany, Italy, Belgium, and the Netherlands. He also included in the proposal to ban the Soviet shorter range nuclear missiles with ranges in excess of 300 miles (500 kilometers). With regard to the British and French nuclear forces, General Secretary Gorbachev abandoned his demand for elimination of weapons now deployed but called for a pledge not to increase them.

At their second summit meeting in **Reykjavík, Iceland** in the fall of 1986, the two leaders discussed the elimination of all nuclear ballistic missiles, but differences over SDI blocked any arms control progress.

Finally, on December 8, 1987, at the third Reagan-

Gorbachev summit meeting held in **Washington,** the United States and the Soviet Union agreed to unprecedented on-site inspection verification measures and signed the **INF Treaty** obligating both parties to eliminate all their intermediate-range and shorter-range missile systems within three years. The treaty was ratified by Congress in the spring of 1988.

The Reagan administration changed the name of SALT to **START,** the Strategic Arms **Reduction** Talks. Negotiations resumed in June 1982. The Reagan opening proposal called for substantial cuts in ballistic missiles and their warheads, particularly on land-based ICBMs where the Soviets placed about 70 percent of their strategic resources. However, the proposal did not require the United States to cancel any of the planned improvements in its strategic weapons systems—the MX missiles, the Trident I and Trident II submarine-launched ballistic missiles, and the B-1 bomber. Moreover, this proposal would have permitted an increase in U.S.-deployed warheads due to the placement of several thousand cruise missiles on strategic bombers, submarines, and surface ships.

START Talks

The initial Soviet proposal at START suggested that reductions be carried out in categories of forces previously established in the SALT II negotiations. However, the Kremlin stated that reductions along these lines were contingent upon a satisfactory solution to the INF talks—in other words, no Pershing II and cruise missile deployments.

The United States then revised its START position in several respects. The previously suggested limitations on Soviet land-based ICBMs were eased somewhat. Then, in 1983, President Reagan agreed to offer the Kremlin a **build-down** proposal, as suggested by a bipartisan group in Congress. In return, these members of Congress agreed to support the MX missile.

build-down

The "build-down" idea proposed that new weapons could continue to be developed and deployed as long as a greater number of warheads in the existing forces was retired. Separate ratios were proposed for different categories of nuclear weapons: e.g., 2 MIRVed ICBMs were to be retired for every new one deployed; 3 MIRVed SLBMs retired for every 2 new ones deployed; and one single-warhead missile retired for every new one deployed.

The Soviet Union objected to the "build-down" proposal as another means to cut deeply into its land-based missile forces. Like the INF talks, the START negotiations were clearly deadlocked by the winter of 1983.

Both President Reagan and Secretary of Defense Weinberger proclaimed, as did their predecessors, that there could be no winners in a nuclear war. Yet a Defense Department document—Defense Guidance 1984–1988—announced the strategy that "should deterrence fail and strategic war with the Soviet Union occur, the United States must have the forces that can prevail."

Strategic Defense Initiative (SDI)

Expressing his dissatisfaction with the concept of deterrence through mutual vulnerability and the progress of arms control, President Reagan, in March 1983, proposed an intensive research and development program to render nuclear weapons "impotent and obsolete." This **Strategic Defense Initiative** contemplated a space-based system and thus was promptly

"Star Wars" dubbed **Star Wars.**

Consideration had been given to the creation of a defense against nuclear missiles in the previous administrations of Presidents Kennedy, Johnson, and Nixon, but it was always concluded that such systems could not provide protection from a large-scale enemy attack.

The announced purpose of the Reagan space-based Strategic Defense Initiative, or "Star Wars," was to defend the United States against land-based intercontinental ballistic missiles and submarine-launched ballistic missiles. However, it does not purport to be designed to defend against Soviet bombers and Soviet cruise missiles carrying thousands of nuclear warheads.

Since testing and deployment of a space-based SDI would be a repudiation of the 1972 Anti-Ballistic Missile Treaty, the Reagan administration considered the possible withdrawal from all or part of the **ABM Treaty.** One of the grounds cited was that an uncompleted Soviet radar installation, located near Krasnoyarsk in south central Russia, was not only a treaty violation but could be considered a "material breach" of the accord because it is not located on the Soviet periphery. The Soviet Union denied the allegation but stopped construction in 1987.

To transform the complaint into a "formal assertion" would give the United States a legal right to withdraw from the accord. The Joint Chiefs of Staff and Secretary of State George Shultz rejected this proposal and favored maintaining the treaty's obligation, while others in the administration favored heightening its complaint about this radar.

The Soviets argued that proponents of this proposal were attempting to provide "a comfortable option" to deploy comprehensive ballistic missile defenses in violation of the ABM accord.

At their **Moscow** summit in June 1988, their fourth and final meeting, Soviet leader Mikhail Gorbachev told President Reagan that the Krasnoyarsk radar would be dismantled if the superpowers reached an agreement on the missile defense issue. Reagan told Gorbachev that an agreement reducing strategic arms could not be reached if the radar was not dismantled.

SALT I and SALT II agreements limiting offensive arms have officially expired (SALT II was never ratified). President Reagan said that he would do nothing to undercut or jeopardize these agreements so long as the Soviet Union exercised similar restraint. However, the Reagan administration voiced concern over Soviet compliance with these and other agreements.

In order to stay within the SALT II ceiling on MIRVed ballistic missiles, President Reagan decided to dismantle an older Poseidon ballistic missile submarine in 1985 when a new Trident submarine went on sea trials. However, due to alleged Soviet violations, pressures continued for a "proportionate response."

In late 1986, President Reagan announced that the United States would no longer voluntarily abide by the SALT II limitations and in fact exceeded the limit of 1320 on the combined total of MIRVed ballistic missile launchers and strategic bombers with long-range cruise missiles. Subsequent retirement of ballistic missile submarines and Congressional resistance have, however, resulted in substantial adherence to the treaty terms.

Since the beginning of the nuclear age, each side has continued to develop new systems that pose even greater threats to the other's forces. Technology continues to outpace the process of arms control.

The arms control talks proceed. . . .

1989 · The Bush Years

"Let us have a kinder, gentler nation."

George Bush
January 20, 1989

In the early days of his administration, President George Bush made certain modifications in the defense and arms control policies of his predecessor. He announced that a review would be undertaken of the U.S. strategic force posture and negotiating position in the *START Talks.* He also suggested that greater emphasis would be given to reducing conventional forces and eliminating chemical weapons.

Recognizing budgetary constraints, he reduced the proposed Reagan defense expenditures by billions of dollars and scaled down the *Strategic Defense Initiative (Star Wars)* to a more realistic level. At the same time, however, he asked Congress to fund two mobile ICBMs: a rail-based MX and the single-warhead Midgetman to be deployed on trucks.

President Bush inherited unprecedented activity in the arms control field including the talks on strategic and spaced-based systems, verification of nuclear testing limits, a new approach to limiting conventional weaponry, and elimination of chemical weapons.

Despite the progress made by the Reagan administration, President Bush still had to deal with such issues as the reconciliation of SDI and confirmed compliance with the 1972 Anti-Ballistic Missile Treaty; the constraints on sea-based nuclear-tipped cruise missiles; and the status of mobile ICBMs. When the *START Talks* resumed in June 1989, agreement in principle had been reached on an approximately 30 percent overall cut in U.S. and Soviet nuclear arsenals.

Midgetman

MX

The President's decision to deploy two mobile U.S. missiles—the truck-mounted Midgetman and the rail-based MX—was in direct conflict with the U.S. negotiating position that the U.S. and Soviet powers should ban mobile ICBMs, such as the Soviet ten-warhead SS-24 and the single-warhead SS-25.

One solution under consideration was to ban just multiple-warhead mobile missiles, such as the SS-24 and MX deployment on rail cars, while allowing a specified number of single-warhead SS-25s and Midgetmen. Some officials argued that the plan could be presented as a two-track decision: the U.S. would deploy the MX aboard rail cars unless MIRVed mobile missiles were banned in a new accord. But President Bush and Secretary of Defense Richard Cheney have continued to say that mobile deployment of the ten-warhead MX should be given top priority.

Moreover, Bush's statements made during his candidacy and early in his administration suggested that START might not be given the high priority that it had under Reagan. Bush showed greater interest in reducing chemical weapons and conventional forces, and some of his key advisors expressed skepticism about the emerging outline of a START treaty. By June 1989, however, President Bush announced the completion of his strategic review and a willingness to proceed in START without major changes. A new wrinkle was the proposal to agree on trial runs on treaty verification measures even before full agreement was reached on substance.

short-range
nuclear
missiles

With the signing and ratification of the INF Treaty, the Reagan administration had committed the United States to major modernization of the remaining European-based nuclear forces, principally the aging **short-range Lance missiles.** Housed in West Germany— NATO's front line—with a range of about 80 miles, the Lance would be replaced with a more powerful and longer range missile by the mid-1990s. The so-called follow-on-to-Lance would have a range just be-low the INF Treaty floor of 300 miles and would be deployed in a number several times that of current Lance deployment.

Prior to the NATO summit in May 1989, the United States and the British government under Prime Minister Margaret Thatcher, a strong proponent of the modernization program, adamantly opposed ngotiations on reducing the short-range missiles. The concern was that such negotiations would inevitably lead to the total elimination of the short-range nuclear missiles, which are all the missiles remaining in NATO's arsenal in the wake of the recent U.S.-Soviet INF Treaty banning intermediate-range arms.

At the urging of several European allies and because of the increasing political turmoil in Germany demanding East-West negotiations on short-range missiles, the Bush administration agreed to forego its attempt to obtain Atlantic alliance agreement for modernization in late 1989.

It was suggested by these European countries that before NATO brings new missiles into Europe, NATO should explore more fully the promise of greater arms reductions held by Gorbachev. It was also suggested that negotiations for lower levels of short-range weapons could be part of a package to reduce conventional forces.

General Secretary Gorbachev announced in December 1988 that the Soviet Union would unilaterally reduce its armed forces by 500,000 men and substantially reduce forward-based tanks and artillery, as well as other elements of surprise-attack capability. *conventional forces*

The United States had 305,000 ground and air force personnel in Europe, including combat and noncombat forces. The Soviet Union had about 725,000 troops outside its territory. President Bush, in May 1989 at the NATO summit, proposed to cut U.S. forces in Europe by 30,000 troops—a 10 percent reduction—if the Soviet Union would cut to the same level of 275,000.

These proposals were overtaken by the rapidly breaking developments in Eastern Europe, with the

Warsaw Pact no longer an effective military alliance. Presidents Bush and Gorbachev agreed to limit the respective forces in Central Europe to 195,000, but with Soviet troop withdrawals from Hungary and Czechoslovakia and budgetary pressures in the United States for a "peace dividend," even greater reductions can be envisaged.

Substantial progress by the Bush administration in several areas of arms control now appears possible. President Bush has also proposed:

- cutting $7 billion from the space-based missile defense program (SDI) by 1992 (and Congress is likely to insist on much deeper cuts);
- delaying the production of the B-2 Stealth Bomber for one year because of concerns over technical problems and the program's expense—132 bombers for a total of $70 billion;
- reducing conventional forces in central Europe to 195,000 for each superpower and an additional 30,000 American troops elsewhere in Europe (the Soviet Union has agreed but the actual levels will undoubtedly be much larger); and
- postponing the modernization of shorter range missiles in Europe (with German unification pending, the modification is effectively dead).

The arms control process continues and broadens. . . .

U.S. Administrations

Timeline years: 1945 · 1950 · 1955 · 1960 · 1965 · 1970 · 1975 · 1980 · 1985 · 1990

1945 • 1952
President
Harry S. Truman
Secretary of State
James Byrnes
George Marshall
Dean Acheson
Secretary of Defense
James Forrestal
Louis Johnson
George Marshall
Robert Lovett
National Security Advisor
Sidney Souers

1953 • 1960
President
Dwight D. Eisenhower
Secretary of State
John Foster Dulles
Christian Herter
Secretary of Defense
Charles Wilson
Neil McElroy
Thomas Gates
National Security Advisor
James Lay

1961 • 1968
President
John F. Kennedy
Secretary of State
Dean Rusk
Secretary of Defense
Robert McNamara
National Security Advisor
McGeorge Bundy
• • •
Lyndon B. Johnson
Secretary of State
Dean Rusk
Secretary of Defense
Robert McNamara
Clark Clifford
National Security Advisor
McGeorge Bundy
Walter Rostow

1969 • 1976
President
Richard Nixon
Secretary of State
Richard Rogers
Henry Kissinger
Secretary of Defense
Melvin Laird
Elliott Richardson
James Schlesinger
National Security Advisor
Henry Kissinger
• • •
Gerald Ford
Secretary of State
Henry Kissinger
Secretary of Defense
James Schlesinger
Donald Rumsfeld
National Security Advisor
Brent Scowcroft

1977 • 1980
President
Jimmy Carter
Secretary of State
Cyrus Vance
Edmund Muskie
Secretary of Defense
Harold Brown
National Security Advisor
Zbigniew Brzezinski

1981 • 1988
President
Ronald Reagan
Secretary of State
Alexander Haig
George Shultz
Secretary of Defense
Caspar Weinberger
Frank Carlucci
National Security Advisor
Richard Allen
William Clark, Jr.
Robert McFarlane
John Poindexter
Colin Powell

1989 •
President
George Bush
Secretary of State
James Baker
Secretary of Defense
Richard Cheney
National Security Advisor
Brent Scowcroft

U.S.S.R Counterparts

Timeline years: 1945 · 1950 · 1955 · 1960 · 1965 · 1970 · 1975 · 1980 · 1985 · 1990

1940s • 1953
General Secretary
Josef Stalin
Foreign Minister
Vyacheslav Molotov
Defense Minister
Josef Stalin
Nikolai Bulganin
Alexander Vasilevskiy

1954 • 1963
General Secretary
Nikita Khrushchev
Foreign Minister
Vyacheslav Molotov
Andrei Gromyko
Defense Minister
Nikolai Bulganin
Georgi Zhukov
Rondion Malinovski

1964 • 1982
General Secretary
Leonid Brezhnev
Foreign Minister
Andrei Gromyko
Defense Minister
Rondion Malinovski
Andrei Grechko
Dimitri Ustinov

1983 • 1985
General Secretary
Yuri Andropov
Konstantin Chernenko
Foreign Minister
Andrei Gromyko
Defense Minister
Dimitmri Ustinov

1985 •
General Secretary
Mikhail Gorbachev
Foreign Minister
Andrei Gromyko
Eduard Shevardnadze
Defense Minister
Sergei Sokolov

U.S.—U.S.S.R.
Strategic Nuclear Weapons Competition

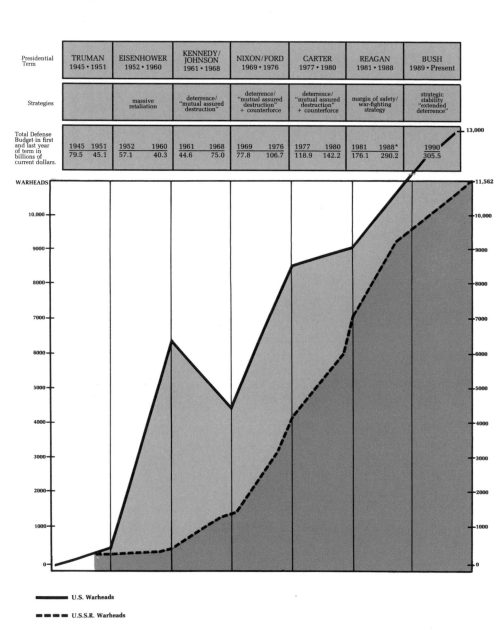

Presidential Term	TRUMAN 1945 • 1951	EISENHOWER 1952 • 1960	KENNEDY/ JOHNSON 1961 • 1968	NIXON/FORD 1969 • 1976	CARTER 1977 • 1980	REAGAN 1981 • 1988	BUSH 1989 • Present
Strategies		massive retaliation	deterrence/ "mutual assured destruction"	deterrence/ "mutual assured destruction" + counterforce	deterrence/ "mutual assured destruction" + counterforce	margin of safety/ war-fighting strategy	strategic stability "extended deterrence"
Total Defense Budget in first and last year of term in billions of current dollars.	1945 1951 79.5 45.1	1952 1960 57.1 40.3	1961 1968 44.6 75.0	1969 1976 77.8 106.7	1977 1980 118.9 142.2	1981 1988* 176.1 290.2	1990 305.5

U.S. Warheads

U.S.S.R. Warheads

Source of Information: "National Defense Budget Estimates FY 1990," *Office of the Assistant Secretary of Defense, Comptroller*, March 1989
*Note: Reagan's request for 1989 was 315.2 billion dollars.

International Concerns

While the United States and the Soviet Union have continued to add to their awesome nuclear stockpiles, the other countries of the world have shown increasing alarm and endeavored to play a part in dealing with this global problem. The multinational **Committee on Disarmament,** which meets regularly in Geneva, attempted to generate agreements on, among other issues, a "comprehensive ban on nuclear testing" and a "prohibition of chemical weapons."

Representatives of these other countries have frequently called the attention of the superpowers to their commitments in the **Treaty on NonProliferation of Nuclear Weapons,** signed in 1968, "to achieve at the earliest possible date the cessation of the nuclear arms race and to undertake effective measures in the direction of nuclear disarmament" and "to seek to achieve the discontinuance of all test explosions of nuclear weapons for all time." The effort to prevent the proliferation of nuclear weapons might well collapse in the absence of progress in bringing the bilateral competition between the United States and the Soviet Union under control.

The United Nations held two special sessions on disarmament in 1978 and 1983, and the seeming indifference of nuclear superpower participation at those sessions was a severe disappointment to supporters of arms control throughout the world.

Impatient with the slow progress of negotiations between the superpowers and frustrated with the inability to translate their concerns into effective measures of arms control, other nations have tried to exert increasing pressure to participate in and expedite the arms control process.

Slow as the process has been, there is no way of achieving arms control that does not involve negotiations between the two nuclear superpowers. Three other countries—Great Britain, France, and the People's Republic of China—are also declared nuclear powers, but their forces are dwarfed by the immense nuclear arsenals of the United States and the Soviet Union. Their inclusion in negotiations directed toward setting ceilings and subceilings on overall nuclear weaponry is unlikely until the U.S. and the U.S.S.R. have made significant progress toward arms reductions.

On the other hand, Great Britain was a full contributing participant in the now-suspended talks seeking a comprehensive ban on the testing of nuclear explosive devices. The participation of France and the People's Republic of China when the talks resume would calm Soviet apprehensions and lead more nations to adhere to the resulting treaty. Global agreement on a cessation of nuclear testing would greatly enhance the prospects for stability and nonproliferation.

Allies of the United States in Western Europe and in the Far East, notably Japan, request and receive regular consultation with U.S. officials on arms control problems. Until completion of the treaty, a major area of concern to the allies involved the intermediate-range nuclear missiles (INF) deployed by the Soviet Union against both European and Asian targets and the U.S. deployment in late 1983 of Pershing II ballistic and ground-launched cruise missiles in Western NATO countries. The Strategic Defense Initiative (SDI or "Star Wars") proposed by President Reagan remains a troubling issue.

In early 1986, when General Secretary Gorbachev called for the elimination of all nuclear weapons by the year 2000, he proposed to eliminate all Soviet SS-20s—the intermediate-range missiles deployed against Europe—in exchange for the elimination of the American Pershing II ballistic missiles and ground-launched cruise missiles stationed in the United Kingdom, Germany, Italy, Belgium, and the Netherlands. He also abandoned his insistence on the elimination of British and French nuclear forces now deployed.

European reaction to the Gorbachev INF proposal was mixed. Although desiring to see a reduction in the Soviet forces specifically designed for use against targets in their countries, some West Europeans regarded the American Pershings and ground-launched cruise missiles as a deterrent to Soviet Union use of what is considered to be its superior conventional forces.

The Japanese expressed concern over any U.S.-Soviet agreement that would leave the Soviet Union free to maintain or even increase the SS-20s aimed at Far Eastern targets.

As the negotiations continued, both sides modified their positions and finally, in December 1987, the United States and the Soviet Union signed the **Intermediate-Range Nuclear Forces Treaty.** The treaty called for the elimination of all intermediate-range nuclear weapons within three years with unprecedented on-site verification procedures. The treaty was ratified in the spring of 1988.

With the signing of the INF Treaty, the concern of the international community was now focused on two remaining unresolved issues: short-range nuclear missiles and conventional forces.

President Bush and Prime Minister Margaret Thatcher of Great Britain—both proponents of a full modernization program to replace the aging Lance short-range missile—encountered strong opposition from several European allies, particularly Germany where the missiles were deployed. The West Germans demanded early East-West negotiations on reduction of short-range missiles.

But President Bush continued to insist on the compromise already reached at the North Atlantic Treaty Organization's 40th Anniversary Summit in Brussels in 1988 that called for reductions in conventional, or nonnuclear, forces before starting talks on the short-range nuclear weapons issue.

To calm the concerns of the European community, President Bush unveiled a conventional arms control proposal at the summit that broke an 18-month impasse in the U.S. position on conventional forces. The Soviet Union wanted to include combat aircraft, armed helicopters, and manpower totals in the complex conventional arms negotiations under way in Vienna. The United States had insisted that aircraft be left for a second phase of the talks after agreement was reached on reductions in tank and artillery strength by both sides. President Bush's proposal stated that these categories should be included in the talks.

France and Britain, however, have refused to allow any of their own nuclear-strike aircraft to become the subject of arms talks with the Soviets.

President Bush strongly stated that significant conventional arms reductions could be accomplished by 1992, thus advancing the possibility of short-range missile negotiations.

In the Pacific, our allies in the **ANZUS treaty**—Australia and New Zealand—exhibit varying degrees of concern about their association with a nuclear superpower. The New Zealand government has refused port visits by nuclear-powered ships, and there are moves to make this a matter of formal legislation. Australia, much more deeply involved in military relations with the United States, has not followed the New Zealand example. However, anti-nuclear groups within Australia continue to exert appreciable political pressure.

Finally, the nonaligned nations, represented by Argentina, Greece, India, Mexico, Sweden and Tanzania, known as the *Delhi Six,* have called for a place at the negotiating table. They enthusiastically supported a Soviet moratorium on nuclear tests intended to lead to a permanent comprehensive test ban. Their intervention gained added significance from the fact that India set off what it claimed to be a test of a peaceful nuclear explosive device in 1973, and Argentina is typically listed among those countries that are approaching the stage of nuclear capability.

Summit Conferences

Although summit conferences are too short to permit detailed negotiations, such meetings are essential to resolve major differences that cannot be handled at lower levels. In addition, U.S. and U.S.S.R. leaders have an opportunity to know one another as individuals rather than ideological abstractions.

Prior to the initiation of the formal strategic arms negotiations, a number of summit conferences dealt peripherally with arms control issues. Beginning in May 1972, when the SALT I agreements were signed, nuclear arms control became the dominant subject.

1955 July   **GENEVA, Switzerland**

> *Participants:*
> United States: President Dwight D. Eisenhower
> Great Britain: Prime Minister Anthony Eden
> France: Premier Edgar Faure
> Soviet Union: Premier Nikolai Bulganin

At this conference, President Eisenhower proposed an "Open Skies" plan calling for inspection of United States' and Soviet territory by aircraft of the respective sides to serve as a warning system against surprise attack. The Soviet Union rejected this plan.

1959 September   **CAMP DAVID, Maryland**

> *Participants:*
> United States: President Dwight D. Eisenhower
> Soviet Union: First Secretary Nikita Khrushchev

At this informal meeting, the leaders touched on questions of nuclear disarmament and the need for peaceful coexistence.

1960 May   **PARIS, France**

> *Participants:*
> United States: President Dwight D. Eisenhower
> Great Britian: Prime Minister Harold MacMillan
> France: President Charles de Gaulle
> Soviet Union: First Secretary Nikita Khrushchev

Before the summit officially opened, Khrushchev demanded an apology for the United States' U-2 "spy plane" flight over the Soviet Union. When Eisenhower refused, Khrushchev walked out of the meeting to show his indignation. This underscored continued Soviet resistance to an "Open Skies" policy.

1961 June   **VIENNA, Austria**

> *Participants:*
> United States: President John F. Kennedy
> Soviet Union: First Secretary Nikita Khrushchev

Among the issues discussed were limits on nuclear testing. The abrasive tone of Khrushchev's remarks caused the meeting to have a negative effect on U.S.-Soviet relations.

1967 June   **GLASSBORO, New Jersey**

> *Participants:*
> United States: President Lyndon B. Johnson
> Soviet Union: Premier Alexei Kosygin

Among the topics covered during this meeting were nuclear proliferation and growing American apprehensions about Soviet ABM plans.

This meeting set the stage for discussions that led to the SALT talks, although the Soviet military intervention in Czechoslovakia delayed their beginning until after President Johnson left office.

1972 May   **MOSCOW, U.S.S.R.**

> *Participants:*
> United States: President Richard Nixon
> Soviet Union: General Secretary Leonid Brezhnev

Notwithstanding President Nixon's May 5th decision to mine the ports of North Vietnam, constituting a threat to Soviet shipping, no ultimatums were issued, and the planned summit went ahead on schedule.

Although the two sides had been close to an agreement on SALT, the summit's main theme, there were several problems that still remained. One concerned a technicality on the ABM (anti-ballistic missile) system and another on land-based mobile ICBMs, which neither country possessed at the time. After long and tedious hours of debate, Nixon and Brezhnev agreed that they would not build land-based mobile ICBMs; but, because of political problems with some of his hardliners, Brezhnev refused to write this promise into the Interim Agreement on Offensive Weapons.

There was a deadlock relating to the number of missile launching submarines each side should be allowed to have. The Kremlin argued that the United States had to include in its numbers the British and French missile launching submarines. President Nixon flatly rejected this inclusion.

Finally the SALT I agreements—the ABM Treaty limiting each

side to two ABM sites and the Interim Agreement limiting offensive nuclear arms—were signed.

The summit concluded with President Nixon and General Secretary Brezhnev signing the twelve-point Basic Principles of Relations between Russia and America symbolizing the end of a two-decade period of hostility and the hoped-for beginning of a new era of restraint and cooperation.

1973 June   WASHINGTON, D.C.

> *Participants:*
> United States: President Richard Nixon
> Soviet Union: General Secretary Leonid Brezhnev

Before President Nixon's visit to Moscow in May 1972, he had invited General Secretary Brezhnev to the United States. In search of American assistance and technology to modernize Russia, Brezhnev was eager to solidify relations with the United States, particularly in view of the new American policy of expanding relations with China.

Unfortunately, however, because of anti-Soviet and anti-Nixon demonstrations, Brezhnev's visit was limited for reasons of security. Nine agreements that Brezhnev had reached with Kissinger prior to the summit were signed one after the other.

President Nixon and General Secretary Brezhnev also set 1974 as the date for completing the SALT II negotiations to limit offensive nuclear weapons and pledged their countries to avoid actions that could lead to nuclear confrontation. It was hoped that these two agreements would be considered historical achievements in that they resulted in ending the Cold War and creating a new period of international relations.

1974 June   MOSCOW, U.S.S.R.

> *Participants:*
> United States: President Richard Nixon
> Soviet Union: General Secretary Leonid Brezhnev

This summit was the last meeting attended by President Nixon.

A Protocol to the ABM Treaty was signed, limiting each country to one anti-ballistic missile site. The Threshold Test Ban Treaty, limiting nuclear weapons test yield to 150 kilotons, was also signed.

1975 November   VLADIVOSTOK, U.S.S.R.

> *Participants:*
> United States: President Gerald Ford
> Soviet Union: General Secretary Leonid Brezhnev

At this summit, agreement was reached on a framework for the

SALT II Treaty, limiting total numbers of missile launchers to 2400 and launchers of MIRVed missiles to 1320.

Issues left ambiguous were the treatment of cruise missiles and the classification of the Backfire bomber as a strategic or theater airplane. However, by reaching a compromise under which the Soviets accepted the principle of equal ceilings and the United States agreed not to insist on selective reduction of Soviet heavy missiles, the two leaders created the framework that led, eventually, to the SALT II Treaty.

1975 July   HELSINKI, Finland

> *Participants:*
> United States: President Gerald Ford
> Soviet Union: General Secretary Leonid Brezhnev

Leaders of the thirty-three nations involved in the Conference on Security and Cooperation in Europe (CSCE), including the two superpowers, signed the Helsinki Declaration, a nonbinding pact on security, economic cooperation, and human rights.

1979 June   VIENNA, Austria

> *Participants:*
> United States: President Jimmy Carter
> Soviet Union: General Secretary Leonid Brezhnev

The two leaders signed the SALT II Treaty limiting U.S. and Soviet strategic offensive nuclear weapons.

Issues discussed included the reduction of forces in Europe (MBFR), anti-satellite weapon negotiations, chemical weapons, and comprehensive test ban negotiations.

Both leaders confirmed their intentions to work for completion of a Comprehensive Test Ban Treaty. This was the first summit conference to involve meetings between the top U.S. and Soviet defense officials, both civilian and military.

1985 November   GENEVA, Switzerland

> *Participants:*
> United States: President Ronald Reagan
> Soviet Union: General Secretary Mikhail Gorbachev

The key issue discussed at this summit was President Reagan's Strategic Defense Initiative (SDI), or Stars Wars. The two leaders spent over five hours in person-to-person conversation. The polarized positions on strategic defense came no closer together. Gorbachev maintained that offensive reductions could not be accepted if the United States proceeded to test and deploy space-based weapons. Reagan argued for his view that both sides should seek ways to render nuclear weapons impotent and obsolete.

It was agreed that further summits would be held in Washington in 1986 and in Moscow in 1987.

1986 October   REYKJAVIK, Iceland

Participants:
United States: President Ronald Reagan
Soviet Union: General Secretary Mikhail Gorbachev

The two leaders launched into an impromptu discussion about eliminating all nuclear ballistic missiles, leaving only air-breathing systems such as aircraft and cruise missiles. The impasse over strategic defense blocked any full exploration of this idea, which had not been thoroughly studied within the U.S. government. Progress was made on START limits, and both sides moved toward an INF compromise, largely based on the U.S. "zero-option" proposal.

1987 December   WASHINGTON, D.C.

Participants:
United States: President Ronald Reagan
Soviet Union: General Secretary Mikhail Gorbachev

The major purpose of the meeting was to sign the completed INF Treaty. The unwillingness of President Reagan to accept constraints on SDI and the refusal of General Secretary Gorbachev to agree to offensive arms cuts in the absence of such constraints forestalled new agreements.

1988 June   MOSCOW, U.S.S.R.

Participants:
United States: President Ronald Reagan
Soviet Union: General Secretary Mikhail Gorbachev

The final Reagan-Gorbachev summit provided photo opportunities and a demonstration of warmer superpower relations. No real breakthroughs were expected, and none occurred.

1989 November   MALTA HARBOR

Participants:
United States: President George Bush
Soviet Union: General Secretary Mikhail Gorbachev

At this first summit meeting, President Gorbachev proposed and President Bush agreed that the NATO and Warsaw Pact leaders should meet in Geneva before the end of 1990 to sign an agreement limiting conventional armed forces in Europe. They also set the objective of prompt completion of a START Treaty and anticipated the signing of a bilateral agreement on the destruction of most chemical weapons at the next summit, scheduled for June 1990.

1990 June   **WASHINGTON, D.C.**

Participants:
    United States: President George Bush
    Soviet Union: General Secretary Mikhail Gorbachev

Much of President George Bush's and President Mikhail Gorbachev's discussion had to do with the unification of Germany and future German membership in NATO; but arms control was also an important agenda item.

The two leaders signed an agreement providing for drastic cuts in chemical weapons stockpiles and halting any further production of poison gas. They also agreed on the basic provision of a START Treaty but were unable to resolve their differences on testing and modernization of the Soviet SS-18 heavy missile and the inclusion of the Soviet Backfire bomber under START limits. They committed themselves, however, to sign a START Treaty by the end of 1990.

Section II

- **Characteristics of Nuclear Weapons**

  Destructive Power
  Existing Stockpiles
  Stable Deterrence
  Strategic Stability
  Launch-on-warning
  Launch-under-attack
  False Alarms
  Missiles
  Warheads
  Reentry Vehicles
  Strategic Nuclear Weapons
  Intermediate-range Nuclear Weapons
  Tactical Nuclear Weapons

- **Diagrams**

  Ballistic Missile
  Cruise Missile

  Intercontinental Ballistic Missile (ICBM)
  Submarine-Launched Ballistic Missile (SLBM)
  Heavy or Strategic Bombers

- **Chart of U.S. and U.S.S.R. Strategic Nuclear Arsenals**

- **World Map of Nuclear Weapon Countries,**
  NATO-Warsaw Pact Countries

- **Composition of U.S. and U.S.S.R. Strategic Nuclear Arsenals**

- **Chart of U.S. and U.S.S.R. Intermediate-Range Nuclear Forces**

- **European Map of Intermediate-Range Nuclear Forces**

1862

". . . Someday, science may have the existence of mankind in its power and the human race will commit suicide by blowing up the world."

Henry Adams

1872

". . . It is not probable that war will ever absolutely cease until science discovers some destroying force so simple in its administration, so horrible in its effects, that all art, all gallantry will be at an end, and battles will be massacres which the feelings of mankind will be unable to endure."

W. Winwood Reade

1942

". . . As soon as men decide that all means are permitted to fight an evil, then their good becomes indistinguishable from the evil that they set out to destroy."

Christopher Dawson

1947

". . . If I had known that the Germans would not succeed in constructing the atom bomb, I would never have lifted a finger."

Albert Einstein

Characteristics of Nuclear Weapons

Almost fifty years after the first nuclear explosion, the control of nuclear arms has become the most essential element in American foreign policy. For the first time in history two nations, the United States and the Soviet Union, have achieved the means to inflict near-instantaneous and catastrophic destruction on each other and the rest of the world. Several other nations have gained the capability to build and acquire nuclear weapons although on a scale far below that of the superpowers.

Some nuclear weapons have greater explosive power than all the bombs dropped in World War II. The two bombs used in the devastation of Hiroshima and Nagasaki each had the explosive force of 13,000 tons of conventional TNT. Today, even the smallest strategic nuclear weapon carries many times the explosive power of the two weapons that destroyed these Japanese cities. We no longer talk of hundreds or thousands of tons, but of megatons—millions of tons. *destructive power*

1 ton	=	2,000 pounds
1 kiloton	=	1,000 tons or 2,000,000 pounds
1 megaton	=	1,000 kilotons or 1,000,000 tons or 2,000,000,000 pounds

The United States has a current **stockpile** of nuclear weapons estimated to have the destructive power of several thousand megatons distributed in approximately 26,000 nuclear warheads of all kinds. The Soviet Union's stockpile of nuclear weapons is believed to be of somewhat smaller size, but with even more megatons. A conservative calculation predicts that 400 megatons would be sufficient to destroy most of an adversary's industrial base and immediately kill hundreds of millions of people. *existing stockpiles*

stable deterrence

Most observers believe a major conflict between the superpowers has been avoided because both have recognized the catastrophic consequences of a nuclear confrontation. Technology today provides each nation with the capability to maintain a sufficiently large, diverse, and survivable strategic nuclear force to dissuade the adversary from nuclear attack. Threatened with catastrophic retaliation, neither power has the incentive to utilize its nuclear arsenal in a crisis situation. This stalemate between the arsenals of destruction is referred to as a situation of **stable deterrence.**

strategic stability

Despite the huge size of the nuclear arsenals, there is no guarantee that the condition of "stable deterrence" will remain in effect. As technology has progressed, nuclear weapons have become increasingly accurate and thus increasingly threatening to the other side. The resulting insecurity has led both sides to continue to arm themselves with still more sophisticated weapons. Increased vulnerabilities have also led to fears of an increased probability that a nuclear exchange could start. Strategic stability is a balance of forces whereby neither side feels threatened and where pressures to arm are decreased. But this condition of **strategic stability** may not survive in the absence of negotiated restrictions on new nuclear weapons.

launch-on-warning

If the nuclear arms race continues uncontrolled, the increased accuracy of nuclear weapons may alter the conditions of stable deterrence. As each side's forces become increasingly vulnerable, the impulse to use weapons rather than risk losing them will become greater, especially at a time of great crisis when there are indications of military preparations on both sides. This is described as a **launch-on-warning** strategy.

launch-under-attack

Almost as grave a risk would be created by a strategy of **launch-under-attack.** This would involve the launch of nuclear weapons on first indication from satellites and other warning systems that the other side's missiles were headed for its targets in the United States or the Soviet Union. This warning could be the result of a computer malfunction. There have been numerous **false alarms** based on computer malfunctions.

With a situation of strategic stability, in which each side is confident of the survivability of its retaliatory forces and comfortable with the military balance, these dangerous doctrines need not be contemplated.

False Alarms—A report prepared by the Senate Armed Services Committee attests to 3703 alarms from January 1979 to June 1980 that were routinely assessed and dismissed; but 147 false alarms were so serious that they required evaluation as to whether they represented a potential attack.

In 1979, an operator mistake at NORAD headquarters inside Cheyenne Mountain in Colorado transmitted and relayed to NORAD fighter bases an erroneous message—*The United States was under nuclear attack.* Ten fighters from three separate bases in the United States and Canada were scrambled and set airborne; U.S. missile and submarine bases across the nation automatically switched to a higher level of alert.

In 1980, a failed 46-cent chip in a minicomputer relayed a similar message, and this time 100 B-52 bombers were readied for takeoff as was the President's emergency aircraft. In the Pacific, the airborne command post took off from its base in Hawaii.

Missiles, Warheads, Reentry Vehicles

A **nuclear weapon** is an explosive device that uses the power of the atom. Enormous power is released by either the splitting apart (fission) or fusing together (fusion) of atomic nuclei.

Atomic weapons, created by the United States during the Second World War, were based on the principle of fission. Hydrogen weapons were developed by the United States in 1952 and utilize fusion as well as fission. Both are commonly referred to as nuclear weapons, although most weapons built today are hydrogen weapons.

A **missile** is a vehicle that can deliver an **explosive device** (warhead) to a target from distances up to thousands of miles.

The two general types of missiles are:

Ballistic Missile—a missile that is fired into a trajectory or path outside the earth's atmosphere and is then pulled down on its targets under the influence of gravity.

Cruise Missile—a pilotless airplane, about 20 feet long, with wings, a tail, a jet engine, and a computer that acts as a pilot. Cruise missiles fly low adjusting to the terrain, are hard to spot on radar, and are considered to be extremely accurate.

A **warhead** contains the fuse and materials that create the atomic explosion. In the case of a ballistic missile, the warhead is mounted on the front end within the nose cone that constitutes the reentry vehicle.

A **reentry vehicle (RV)** is that portion of the missile that carries and houses the warhead. It is propelled beyond the earth's atmosphere; at the end of its flight, it **reenters** the earth's atmosphere and hits the target.

Some ballistic missiles carry only one reentry vehicle; others carry several, each of which can be directed with high accuracy to widely separated targets. These latter are known as **MIRVs.**

MIRV—Multiple
      Independently-targetable
      Reentry
      Vehicle

Large ballistic missiles can carry ten or more warheads.
Cruise missiles have single warheads only.

The three most commonly recognized categories of nuclear weapons, according to progressively decreased ranges, are:

- **STRATEGIC NUCLEAR WEAPONS**
- **INTERMEDIATE-RANGE NUCLEAR WEAPONS**
- **TACTICAL** or **BATTLEFIELD NUCLEAR WEAPONS**

Ballistic Missile

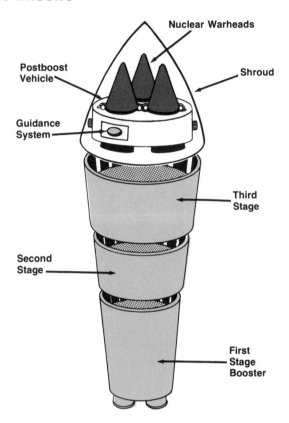

- Nuclear Warheads
- Postboost Vehicle
- Shroud
- Guidance System
- Third Stage
- Second Stage
- First Stage Booster

Trajectory (Path)

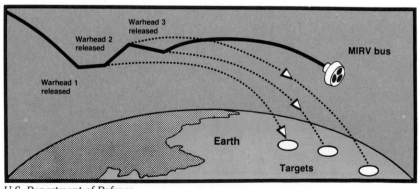

- Warhead 3 released
- Warhead 2 released
- Warhead 1 released
- MIRV bus
- Earth
- Targets

U.S. Department of Defense

Cruise Missile

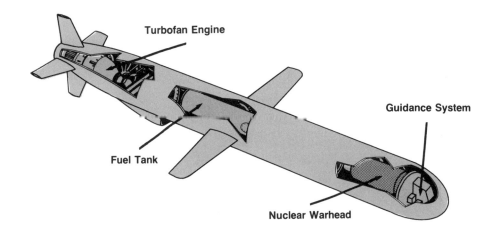

Turbofan Engine

Guidance System

Fuel Tank

Nuclear Warhead

Trajectory (Path)

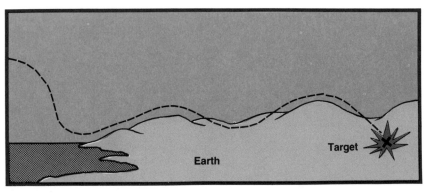

Target

Earth

U.S. Department of Defense

54

Strategic Nuclear Weapons are weapons that, when launched from either the U.S. or the U.S.S.R., have sufficient range to destroy military, industrial, and urban targets in the other side's homeland.

The three principal strategic weapons systems with sufficient range to reach Soviet and American targets are:

ICBMs—Intercontinental Ballistic Missiles
SLBMs—Submarine-Launched Ballistic Missiles
Heavy or **Strategic Bombers**—Aircraft of intercontinental range

These three strategic nuclear weapons form what is called the *triad*—the three forces that deter nuclear attack.

Intercontinental Ballistic Missiles (ICBMs), Submarine-Launched Ballistic Missiles (SLBMs), and **Heavy** or **Strategic Bombers** are defined on the following pages. A chart indicates the number of missiles, warheads, and megatonnage in the arsenals of the United States and the Soviet Union.

I C B M—Inter
Continental
Ballistic
Missile

An **ICBM** is a land-based rocket-propelled vehicle capable of inter-continental range in excess of 4000 nautical miles. It is presently stored or housed in a **silo**, a vertical underground launcher. Deployment of ICBMs on mobile launchers is under consideration by both superpowers.

The United States and the Soviet Union arsenals consist of the following ICBMs*:

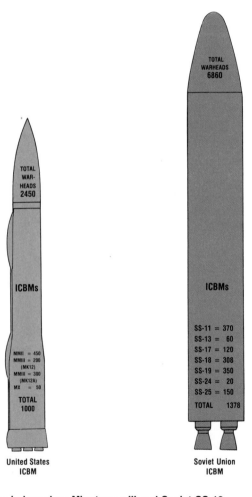

United States
ICBM

Soviet Union
ICBM

*Comparative size is based on Minuteman III and Soviet SS-19

S L B M—Submarine
Launched
Ballistic
Missile

An **SLBM** is a ballistic missile launched from a submarine either sur-faced or submerged. It is stored, or housed, and launched from a **tube**.

The United States and the Soviet Union arsenals consist of the following types of SLBMs*:

TOTAL
WARHEADS

3602

TOTAL
WARHEADS

5312

SLBMs

SLBMs

SS-N-6 = 240
SS-N-8 = 286
SS-N-17 = 12
SS-N-18 = 224
SS-N-20 = 100
SS-N-23 = 64

POSEIDON = 224
TRIDENT   = 384

TOTAL   608

TOTAL   926

United States
SLBM

Soviet Union
SLBM

*Comparative size is based on Trident I and Soviet SS-N-18

Heavy or Strategic Bomber

A **Heavy Bomber** is a military aircraft designed to deliver nuclear or non-nuclear weapons against targets on the ground. The Heavy Bomber can fly strategic missions at intercontinental distances.

Weapons that can be carried by U.S. Heavy Bombers are:

Nuclear Gravity Bombs—a nuclear device designed to be carried by aircraft and released over its target without independent means of propulsion.

SRAMs—Short-Range Attack Missiles—a guided missile with a range of approximately 75 miles.

ALCMs—Air-Launched Cruise Missiles—a long-range guided missile whose flight path remains within the earth's atmosphere.

ASBMs—Air-to-Surface Ballistic Missiles—a missile that, when launched from an airplane, would be capable of reaching a target from distances up to thousands of miles. No ASBMs have been developed and deployed.

The United States and the Soviet Union arsenals consist of the following strategic bombers:

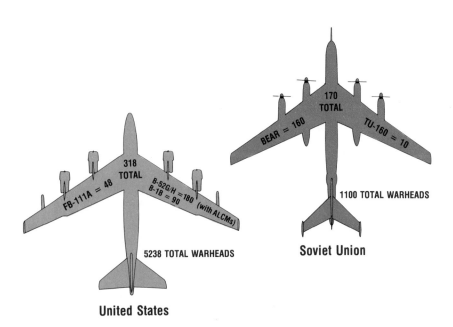

Total U.S. Strategic Nuclear Arsenal

Strategic Systems	Number of Launchers	Warheads per Launcher	Total Warheads	Yield in MT. per Warhead	Total Megatons
ICBMs					
Minuteman II	450	1	450	1.200	540.0
Minuteman III					
Mk-12	200	3	600	.170	102.0
Mk-12A	300	3	900	.335	301.5
MX/Peacekeeper	50	10	500	.300	150.0
Total ICBMs	1000		2450		1093.5
SLBMs					
Poseidon C-3	224	10	2240	.050	112.0
Trident 1 C-4	384	8	3072	.100	307.2
Total SLBMs	608		5312		419.2
HEAVY or STRATEGIC BOMBERS					
B-1B	90	SRAMs; bombs	1614	.150	242.1
B-52G/H	180	SRAMs; bombs; ALCMs	1140	.170	193.8
FB-111A	48	SRAMs; bombs	2484	.500	1242.0
Total Bombers	318		5238		1677.9
Grand Total	1926		13,000		3190.6

Total U.S.S.R. Strategic Nuclear Arsenal

Strategic Systems	Number of Launchers	Warheads per Launcher	Total Warheads	Yield in MT. per Warhead	Total Megatons
ICBMs					
SS-11					
M2	160	1	160	1.10	176.0
M3	210	3	630	.35	220.5
SS-13 M2	60	1	60	.75	45.0
SS-17 M3	120	4	480	.75	360.0
SS-18 M4	308	10	3080	.55	1694.0
SS-19 M3	350	6	2100	.55	1155.0
SS-24	20	10	200	.55	110.0
SS-25	150	1	150	.55	82.5
Total ICBMs	1378		6860		3843.0
SLBMs					
SS-N-6 M3	240	2	480	1.00	480.0
SS-N-8 M1/M2	286	1	286	1.50	429.0
SS-N-17	12	1	12	1.00	12.0
SS-N-18 M1-3	224	7	1568	.50	784.0
SS-N-20	100	10	1000	.20	200.0
SS-N-23	64	4	256	.10	25.6
Total SLBMs	926		3602		1930.6
HEAVY or STRATEGIC BOMBERS					
Tu-95—Bear A	15	2 bombs	30	3.00	90.0
Tu-95—Bear B/C	25	4 bombs	100	1.25	125.0
Tu-95—Bear G	45	6 bombs	270	.68	184.0
Tu-142—Bear H	75	8 bombs	600	.25	150.0
Tu-160	10	10 bombs	100	.50	50.0
Total Bombers	170		1100		599.0
Grand Total	2474		11,562		6372.6

Source of Information: "Military Posture Statement for Fiscal 1989," Joint Chiefs of Staff; *The Military Balance 1988-1989*, International Institute for Strategic Studies; "Nuclear Weapons Data Book—Volume IV," Natural Resources Defense Council; "Annual Reports," U.S. Department of Defense

ARCTIC OCEAN

GREENLAND

ICELAND

EAST GERMA

NETHERLANDS

WEST GERMANY

DE

GREAT BRITAIN

IRELAND

BELGIUM
LUXEMBOURG
FRANCE
SWITZERLAND
AUSTRIA

PORTUGAL

SPAIN

MOROCCO

ALG

ALASKA

CANADA

UNITED STATES

ATLANTIC OCEAN

MEXICO

CUBA

VENEZUELA

PACIFIC OCEAN

COLOMBIA

PERU

BRAZIL

CHILE

ARGENTINA

NATO[1] Countries

Warsaw Pact Countries

Countries with Nuclear Weapons

Countries openly interested in Nuclear Weapons

Countries with probable Nuclear Weapons Capability

[1]North Atlantic Treaty Organization

World Map of: Nuclear Weapons Countries
NATO and Warsaw Pact Countries

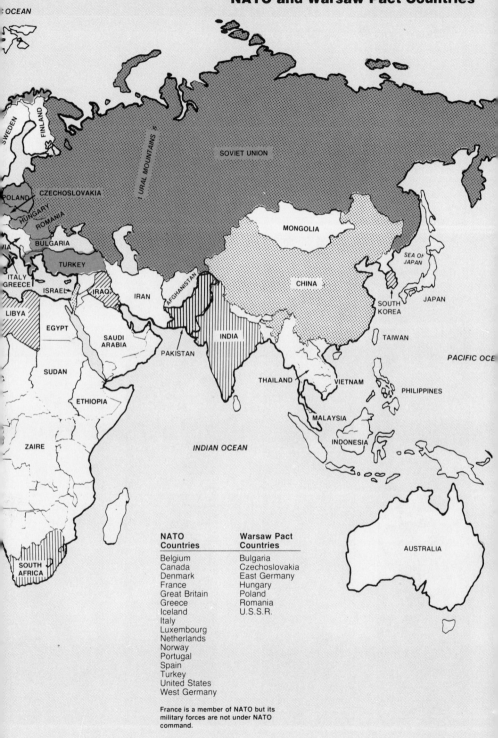

NATO
Countries

Belgium
Canada
Denmark
France
Great Britain
Greece
Iceland
Italy
Luxembourg
Netherlands
Norway
Portugal
Spain
Turkey
United States
West Germany

Warsaw Pact
Countries

Bulgaria
Czechoslovakia
East Germany
Hungary
Poland
Romania
U.S.S.R.

France is a member of NATO but its
military forces are not under NATO
command.

Composition of U.S. and U.S.S.R. Strategic Arsenals

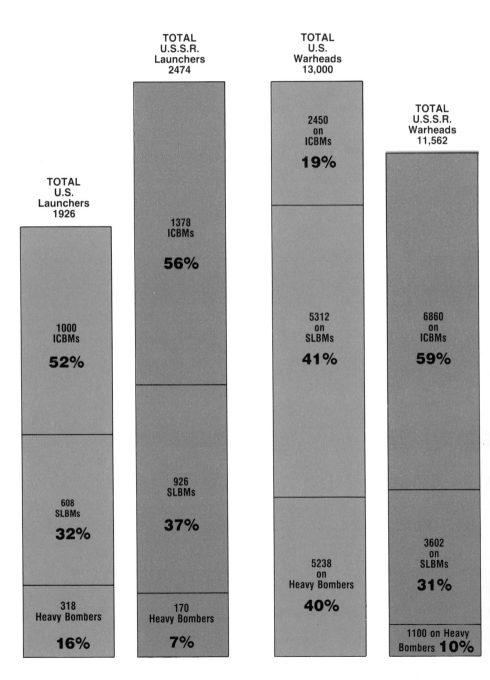

TOTAL
U.S.S.R.
Launchers
2474

TOTAL
U.S.
Warheads
13,000

TOTAL
U.S.S.R.
Warheads
11,562

TOTAL
U.S.
Launchers
1926

2450
on
ICBMs
19%

1378
ICBMs
56%

1000
ICBMs
52%

5312
on
SLBMs
41%

6860
on
ICBMs
59%

926
SLBMs
37%

608
SLBMs
32%

5238
on
Heavy Bombers
40%

3602
on
SLBMs
31%

318
Heavy Bombers
16%

170
Heavy Bombers
7%

1100 on Heavy
Bombers **10%**

Intermediate-Range Nuclear Weapons—also known as Long-Range ***Theater*** Nuclear Weapons—are of longer range, 1000 to 2500 miles, and larger yield than a Tactical or Battlefield Nuclear Weapon.

Intermediate-range nuclear weapons have become increasingly accurate and can be delivered by land-based missiles, submarines and surface ships, as well as by aircraft.

The following chart and map indicate the ***intermediate-range nuclear weapons*** deployed in Europe by the United States and allied forces and the Soviet Union and Warsaw Pact forces. As a result of the INF Treaty, all land-based INF missiles, as well as all other missiles with ranges in excess of 300 miles, are being eliminated.

Tactical or ***Battlefield Nuclear Weapons (TACNUCS)***—are short-range, typically 100 miles or less, low-yield (usually well below 100,000 tons of TNT) nuclear weapons designed for combat use on the battlefield. These weapons cannot reach rearguard forces of the opponent or the opponent's homeland.

NATO contemplates use of such weapons to defeat a massive conventional attack by Warsaw Pact forces. Within NATO, however, they remain in the hands of U.S. forces only. Soviet forces are similarly equipped.

"For with the advent of atomic weapons, we have come either to the last page of war or to the last page of history."

B.H. Liddell Hart

Intermediate-Range Nuclear Forces (after Implementation of INF Treaty)
U.S. and Allied Forces

Systems	Number of Launchers	Warheads Bombs	Total Bombs Warheads	Range in Miles	Countries Based-In
IRBM					
SSBS S/3 (French)	18	1	18	2188	France
SLBM					
Polaris A3 (British)	64	3*	192	2875	Britain
MSBS M-20 (French)	64	1	64	1875	France
MSBS M-4 (French)	32	6	192	3750	France
Total Cruise/Ballistic Missiles	178		466		

*Multiple warheads but not separately targetable

Systems	Number of Launchers	Warheads Bombs	Total Bombs Warheads	Range in Miles	Countries Based-In
Land-Based Aircraft					
F-111 E/F (U.S.)	165	2	330	2938	Britain
F-16 A B C D (U.S.)	300	1	300	1688	Bel./Neth. W. Germany
F-104 (NATO)*	180	1	180	1625	NATO
Mirage IVP (French)	18	1	18	1875	France
Mirage 2000 (French)	15	1	15	950	France
Jaguar (French)	45	1	45	938	France
Mirage 111E (French)	15	1	15	750	
Buccaneer (British)	25	1	25	2125	Britain
Tornado Bomber (British)	220	1	220	1625	Brit./Italy W. Germany
Carrier-Based Aircraft					
A-6E (U.S.)	20	2	40	2000	U.S. carrier
A-7E (U.S.)	24	2	48	1750	U.S. carrier
Super Etendard (French)	36	1	36	813	France
F/A-18 Hornet	24	1	24	660	U.S. carrier
Total Air-delivered Weapons	1087		1296		

*Being replaced by F-16 & Tornado

NATO Totals	**1658**		**2155**		

U.S.S.R.–Warsaw Pact (after Implementation of INF Treaty)

Aircraft				
Backfire	175	2	350	5000
TU-16 Badger	287	2	574	3000
TU-22 Blinder	136	2	272	1375
SU-24 Fencer	600	2	1200	2500
SU-17 Fitter	650	1	650	1125
MIG27 Flogger D	550	1	550	875
MIG21 Fishbed	100	1	100	688
MIG23 Flogger	1000	1	1000	1625
Total Air-Delivered Weapons	3498		4696	
Warsaw Pact Totals	**3498**		**4696**	

Source of Information: "Military Posture Statement for Fiscal 1989," Joint Chiefs of Staff; *The Military Balance 1988-1989*, International Institute for Strategic Studies; "Nuclear Weapons Data Book—Volume IV," Natural Resources Defense Council; "Annual Reports," U.S. Department of Defense

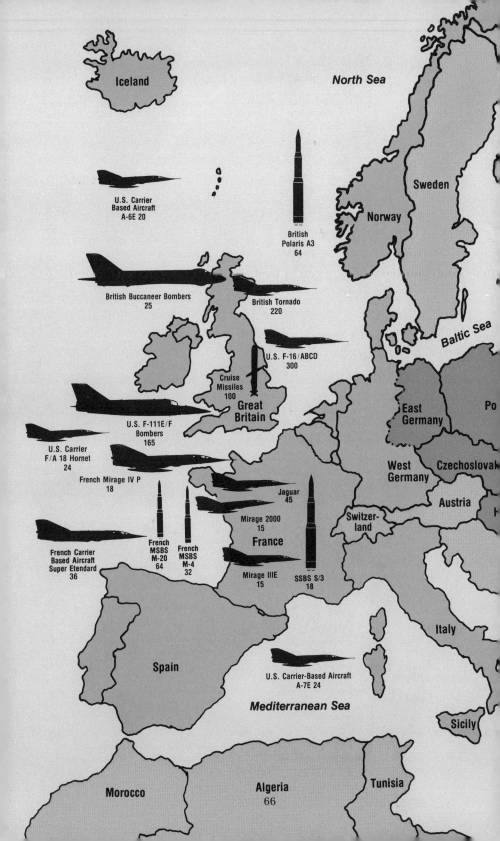

Iceland

North Sea

U.S. Carrier
Based Aircraft
A-6E 20

British
Polaris A3
64

Sweden

Norway

British Buccaneer Bombers
25

British Tornado
220

Baltic Sea

U.S. F-16/ABCD
300

Cruise
Missiles
100

Great
Britain

East
Germany

Po

U.S. F-111E/F
Bombers
165

U.S. Carrier
F/A 18 Hornet
24

West
Germany

Czechoslovak

French Mirage IV P
18

Jaguar
45

Austria

French
MSBS
M-20
64

French
MSBS
M-4
32

Mirage 2000
15

Switzer-
land

French Carrier
Based Aircraft
Super Etendard
36

France

Mirage IIIE
15

SSBS S/3
18

Italy

Spain

U.S. Carrier-Based Aircraft
A-7E 24

Mediterranean Sea

Sicily

Morocco

Algeria

Tunisia

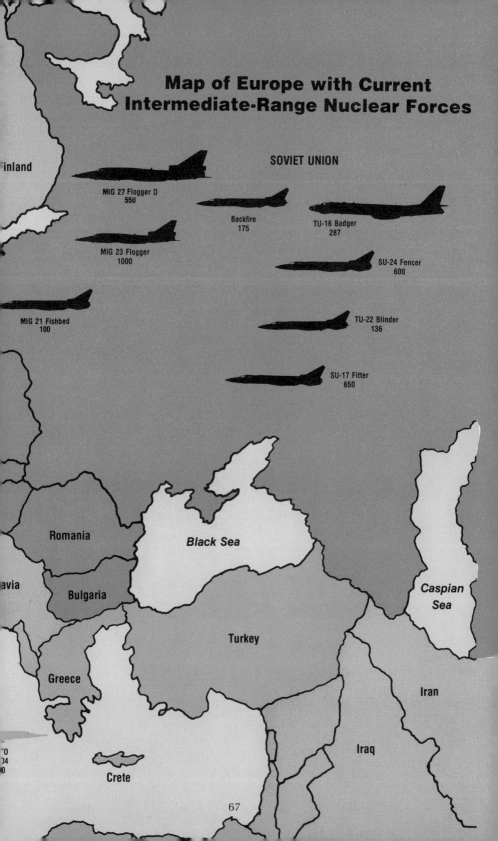

Map of Europe with Current Intermediate-Range Nuclear Forces

SOVIET UNION

Finland

MIG 27 Flogger D
550

Backfire
175

TU-16 Badger
287

MIG 23 Flogger
1000

SU-24 Fencer
600

MIG 21 Fishbed
100

TU-22 Blinder
136

SU-17 Fitter
650

Romania

Black Sea

avia

Bulgaria

Caspian
Sea

Turkey

Greece

Iran

Iraq

Crete

I C B M from Launch Pad

U.S. Department of Defense

Section III

"If peace and survival are to be achieved, the search must almost certainly go beyond the effort to find a balance in thermal nuclear terror."

John Kenneth Galbraith

"Since wars begin in the minds of men, it is in the minds of men that the defenses of peace must be constructed."

Anonymous
Quoted in the UNESCO
Constitution

U.S. Offensive Weapons Systems

Nuclear weapons systems with sufficient range to reach targets either in the United States or the Soviet Union to initiate an attack or retaliate in the event of one are called *offensive strategic weapons systems.*

The United States and the Soviet Union have structured their strategic forces—*Intercontinental Ballistic Missiles (ICBMs), Submarine-Launched Ballistic Missiles (SLBMs),* and *Heavy or Strategic Bombers* known as the *Triad*—in very different ways, thus making the *strategic balance* very difficult to measure. A situation of overall parity can be distorted by looking at one possible criterion and ignoring others.

Some consider the most important measure of relative strength to be the number of *warheads.* Others consider *megatonnage,* the explosive force available on either side, to be the most important criterion of nuclear strength. The United States leads in warheads; the Soviet Union leads in megatonnage.

Since the late 1950s, the United States has opted to build smaller, solid-fueled, land-based missiles and to place the largest share of its warheads on relatively invulnerable submarines. In addition, the United States has always maintained a large bomber force.

The Soviet Union chose to take a different course. The Soviets have long emphasized land-based missiles. Their missiles are much larger in dimension and in number. In addition, they have built a large number of missile-carrying submarines. The Soviets have chosen not to build a large number of modern intercontinental-range bombers.

Today, most experts agree that the United States leads in long-range bombers, cruise missiles, and missile accuracy, and has better submarine-launched ballistic missiles and missile-carrying submarines. These experts also agree that the Soviets lead in the number of land- and sea-based missiles, the lifting power (or *throw-weight*) of those missiles, the explosive power (megatonnage) of their nuclear weapons, as well as the number of nuclear submarines.

Both sides are currently creating adjuncts to their triads by developing and deploying advanced cruise missiles that can be land-based or carried by submarines, surface craft, and bombers.

MX Missile
(Missile eXperimental)

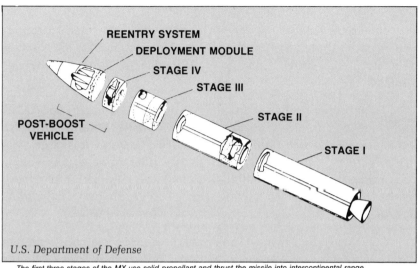

REENTRY SYSTEM

DEPLOYMENT MODULE

STAGE IV

STAGE III

STAGE II

POST-BOOST VEHICLE

STAGE I

U.S. Department of Defense

The first three stages of the MX use solid propellant and thrust the missile into intercontinental range.
The fourth stage, the post-boost vehicle, uses liquid fuel and contains the new and more precise computers, guidance electronics, and communications equipment that control the missile. It is also designed to carry up to 12 independently targetable nuclear reentry vehicles, but current adherence to SALT II provisions will limit testing and deployment of 10 MIRVs.
MX Range—6,900 miles

During the 1980s, the U.S. government decided to improve all three legs of its strategic triad. In his 1980 campaign, Ronald Reagan had warned that the United States was in danger of being surpassed in military strength by the Soviet Union. After his election, President Reagan followed through on his campaign promises by convincing Congress to approve large sums of money for several new strategic nuclear systems.

Land-Based Missiles

The newest American intercontinental ballistic missile (ICBM) is the **MX,** which originally stood for Missile eXperimental when it was first being developed. The MX is officially called the ***Peacekeeper.*** The missile carries ten nuclear warheads known as MIRVs—multiple independently-targetable reentry vehicles. Each warhead can reach a different target; the destination of each warhead can be changed by adjusting the program that the missile is to follow.

The missile itself is 70 feet long, 92 inches in diameter, and weighs approximately 195,000 pounds. Compared with earlier land-based missiles in the U.S. inventory, the MX is more accurate, carries more warheads, and has a greater range and targeting flexibility.

The Soviet Union already has ICBMs larger than the MX, namely, the SS-18. Because of the size and accuracy of these Soviet missiles, many have argued that the United States must match these Soviet capabilities. Others have rejected this idea as placing a "hair trigger" on nuclear war. With each side's forces becoming increasingly accurate and therefore vulnerable to a first strike, they fear that nuclear weapons might be used early in a crisis situation to prevent their being destroyed on the ground.

Development of the MX began in the 1970s, but the question of how the missile should be based created a controversy that continued even after the missile began to be deployed.

Many experts believed the United States should move more of its nuclear forces to basing methods that are less vulnerable to a surprise attack. For land-based missiles such as the MX, it was suggested that the missiles be made mobile since a moving target is more difficult to find and destroy.

In 1972, the Strategic Air Command (SAC) first proposed an advanced ICBM program to replace the **Minuteman** missiles deployed during the Eisenhower and Kennedy administrations. Since then, the Pentagon has been trying to find a basing mode for the MX that would help eliminate the theoretical vulnerability of the U.S. land-based missile force. The goal was to find a method that would be technically feasible, cost-effective, and acceptable to Congress and the public.

Thirty-four different basing options have been studied during the 1970s and 1980s. Deep trenches, railroad tracks, and underwater systems are among the many basing modes considered and rejected by several adminstrations.

In 1979, President Carter announced a decision to go ahead with the MX missile and a complicated **shell game** method—a multiple-basing **race-track** system of deployment. Two hundred missiles would have moved among 4600 shelters in an effort to confuse Soviet military planners.

Subsequently, President Reagan rejected this approach as being too costly while still being vulnerable to a Soviet attack. In November 1982, he announced his intention to base the MX in a configuration known as **Dense Pack**. Located in Wyoming, the Dense Pack field would be a 14-mile long rectangle housing 100 MX missiles spaced 1800 feet apart in silos hardened against nuclear effects.

TRIDENT I

U.S. Department of Defense

In theory, most of the missiles would survive because the Soviets could not time an attack so precisely as to strike all 100 MX silos at the same time. In other words, the combined effects of the blast waves, radiation, and airborne debris caused by the explosion of the first arriving warheads would destroy the latecomers, in what is called a **fratricide** effect.

Congress was unwilling to support this basing plan as it appeared less survivable than the race-track proposal by President Carter. As a result of this impasse, President Reagan appointed a blue-ribbon panel headed by General Brent Scowcroft to review MX basing alternatives and other strategic issues.

The **Scowcroft Commission** finally concluded that 100 MX missiles should be based in the existing Minuteman silos. It also concluded that the threat to U.S. strategic forces by Soviet land-based missiles had been exaggerated. While it was true that the U.S. and Soviet land-based missiles might be vulnerable, U.S. bombers and sea-based missiles remained superior to their Soviet counterparts, and both these legs of the triad could deliver devastating retaliatory blows in the event of a Soviet attack.

The Scowcroft Commission also recommended that the United States proceed to develop a new single-warhead missile that would not pose as much of a threat nor be as attractive a target as the MX. This idea of a small ICBM, or **Midgetman** missile, developed a strong following among members of Congress concerned with defense issues.

In 1985, Congress approved only 50 of the 100 MX missiles proposed by the Pentagon. Any further deployments could come about only if the President proposed and the Congress approved a more survivable basing mode.

In the late 1980s, the Reagan administration and then the Bush administration pushed for a plan whereby MX missiles would be mounted on railroad cars in military bases in the western United States. In the rail-basing plan, MX missiles would be launched from unmarked trains roaming the nation's railways from Arkansas to Washington state.

But Congress was skeptical about the wisdom of a rail-mobile MX. To break this impasse, President Bush endorsed both the mobile MX and the production of the Midgetman nuclear missile, which would be carried on trailers to be towed by trucks with crews of two or three Air Force officers.

STEALTH BOMBER

U.S. Department of Defense

By embracing both of these versions, President Bush hoped to obtain eventual congressional approval of both schemes.

Submarine-Launched Missiles

The United States continued to build up its force of submarine-launched ballistic missiles (SLBMs) during the 1980s. Because U.S. missile-carrying submarines are difficult to find when on patrol in the open seas, the submarine force is generally considered the least vulnerable (or most survivable) leg of America's strategic triad.

The *Trident I or C-4 missile* entered service in 1980. Since that time, this MIRVed SLBM has been deployed on 20 U.S. submarines. Meanwhile, the United States was developing and testing the *Trident II or D-5 missile.* Plans called for the Trident II to become operational in 1990. If the new missile performs as well as expected, it will be the first SLBM accurate enough to threaten well-protected Soviet targets such as hardened missile silos.

Some experts have expressed the concern that because of the Trident II's accuracy, it could be used in a first strike against the Soviet Union and therefore be destabilizing in a crisis. These arguments have failed to gain wide acceptance, however, and the new SLBM appears likely to be deployed on schedule. In addition, during the Reagan years, the United States began stationing nuclear-armed cruise missiles on surface ships and submarines. While these missiles do not have the range of strategic ballistic missiles, they can attack enemy territory from a distance of 2500 kilometers or 1500 miles.

Strategic Bombers

To replace its aging fleet of *B-52* bombers, the United States developed two new bombers in the 1980s. The first, the *B-1B,* became operational in 1986. The intended capability of this supersonic bomber was to penetrate Soviet air defenses. Although 100 have been built, the bomber has been plagued with technical problems, and three crashed during the first year and a half of operation.

The *Stealth Bomber,* also known as the *B-2,* was scheduled to enter the U.S. arsenal in the early 1990s. With a unique "flying wing" shape, a radar-absorbing surface, and advanced electronics, the Stealth is intended to be almost invisible to enemy radar.

In recent years, a growing number of American bombers have also been equipped with long-range *air-launched cruise missiles (ALCMs).* In a U.S.-Soviet conflict, a bomber with ALCMs could attack many targets without having to penetrate the Soviet air defense system.

"... It is vain to look for a defense against lightning."
Maxim 835
Publius Syrus, 1 B.C.

U.S. Defensive Weapons Systems

Certain nuclear weapons systems are intended for defensive purposes only. Because of their short range and other capabilities, these weapons *cannot* be used to initiate an attack or to retaliate against Soviet targets.

In an effort to provide some measure of defense against a nuclear attack, the United States from time to time has made some effort to develop various **defense systems** such as:

- *interceptor aircraft,* equipped with nuclear as well as non-nuclear missiles, to be used to intercept attacking bombers;

- *surface-to-air missiles (SAM),* equipped with nuclear and non-nuclear explosives, to be launched from land and from surface ships against attacking bombers and cruise missiles;

- *anti-submarine warfare (ASW) forces* composed of ships, air-craft, and submarines to be used to detect, identify, track, and destroy hostile missile-carrying submarines; and

- *anti-ballistic missiles (ABM),* to destroy incoming offensive missiles.

With the development of Soviet ballistic missiles, the systems to defend against bomber attack were made obsolete. Incoming ballistic missiles travel at extremely high speeds and are extraordinarily difficult to intercept. Submarines are very difficult to find and to destroy before they launch their missiles. Cruise missiles are extremely difficult to track and shoot down.

In the early 1960s, President Kennedy decided against deployment of the "Nike-Zeus"—an **Anti-Ballistic Missile System** to destroy incoming offensive missiles—when it became clear that the system could not cope with a large-scale enemy attack.

In 1967, President Johnson proposed the "Sentinel" ABM system to protect U.S. cities from accidental or limited nuclear attack, but this program was met with widespread opposition.

In 1969, President Nixon announced a similar program renamed the "Safeguard" ABM system to protect against limited attacks or those aimed at American missile silos.

Because none of the defense weapons are capable of preventing the devastation that would be the inevitable result of a nuclear attack and because no existing technology is adequate to protect against hundreds of missiles carrying thousands of warheads, President Nixon and General Secretary Brezhnev signed the **ABM Treaty** on May 26, 1972, which limited both nations to two ABM sites with no more than 100 missiles each. Subsequently, both sides agreed to reduce the permitted ABM sites to one each. The Treaty was ratified by both countries, is of unlimited duration, and each nation has abided by its terms.

The United States began a "Safeguard" ABM system around the missile silos in Grand Forks, North Dakota. Because of the limited utility of the technology and the expense of operation, it was deactivated a few months later. The Soviets, however, have kept their single permitted ABM system the "Galosh" around Moscow, and it is being replaced by an improved version due to be completed in 1990.

Although deployment of new ABMs is forbidden, research and development programs have continued, and thousands of interceptor aircraft and radar systems have been built. Yet authorities on strategic weaponry are confident that an adversary's bombers and missiles can penetrate any existing or foreseeable defense system, and that it is impossible to build strategic defensive systems capable of keeping casualties to acceptable levels in the event of an attack.

However, President Reagan has expressed the hope that new highly advanced technologies may be found to defend against an attack by nuclear weapons. In March 1983, he proposed a research and development program for a space-based defense system to render nuclear weapons impotent and obsolete. This **Strategic Defense Initiative (SDI)** was characterized **"Star Wars."** Thereafter, an initial five-year, $26 billion research effort was made a part of the proposed defense program.

SDI, or Star Wars, would be intended as a defense against Soviet land-based intercontinental ballistic missiles (ICBMs) and submarine-launched ballistic missiles (SLBMs). In addition to repelling the 10,000 or so Soviet ballistic missile warheads, SDI would have to contend with decoys and other penetration aids, and it would have no capability to deal with non-ballistic nuclear weapons.

To justify the drive toward U.S. development and first-phase deployment of the Strategic Defense Initiative, the Reagan administration argued that the Soviet Union has devoted more resources to strategic defense than the United States, leads the U.S. in some key missile defense technologies, and may be preparing to break out of the Anti-Ballistic Missile Treaty (ABM) and deploy a nationwide missile defense.

Based on the administration's own intelligence estimates, an examination of the Soviet program indicates that while the Soviet programs similar to SDI are active and well-funded, they are not significantly larger than U.S. programs and lag badly in many of the most critical technologies for an effective missile defense. Furthermore, there is no convincing evidence that the Soviet Union is prepared to abandon the ABM Treaty, and there is considerable reason for them not to.

President Reagan's SDI program differed from past ABM systems in that it would be intended to intercept Soviet missiles during all three phases of Soviet missile flight—the **boost phase,** the **mid-course phase** and the **terminal phase.** This is called a **layered defense.** Previous ABM systems sought to deal only with the terminal phase.

The boost phase takes place from the time the missile is launched until it leaves the atmosphere and releases its warheads into space. A missile normally takes one minute to reach outer space and then flies for 2 to 4 minutes before it releases its warheads and decoys. In the boost phase stage, the missile has not released its warheads and decoys, so only one hit is needed to destroy all of them.

After the missile booster drops off, the warheads and decoys begin their flight through outer space, their mid-course phase. The warheads and decoys travel for 20 to 25 minutes before reentering the atmosphere over the target.

As they reenter the atmosphere, the decoys and penetration aids are burned off, and the warheads begin their terminal phase. The terminal phase lasts about 60 seconds, and the warheads can be tracked by ground-based radar.

The theoretical appeal of a layered defense is that it gives the defenses three chances to destroy the attacking missile or warhead instead of one chance. To expand its capabilities to a layered defense, SDI systems might be based in space, or on a mountaintop with mirrors based in space orbits to reflect a lethal beam toward a missile target, or "popped up" into space at the first sign of a Soviet launch.

The defensive weapons now being researched for the Strategic Defense Initiative (SDI) involve futuristic technologies:

X-Ray Lasers are generated by a nuclear explosion in space for use during the *boost phase*. Each explosion would produce dozens of beams approximately 100 feet across destroying anything within their path. Having nuclear devices in orbit would be politically controversial, therefore, it has been proposed by some SDI proponents that mirrors be "popped up" into space after a Soviet attack is detected. Laser beams move in a straight line so the curvature of the earth would force this "pop up" system to be close to the Soviet Union, most likely on a submarine. Because the X-Ray laser would negate President Reagan's goal of non-nuclear defense, it was downplayed in his administration's plans.

Chemical Lasers utilize the reaction of two common chemicals to produce a lethal beam of very intense light that can travel thousands of miles in the blink of an eye. Envisioned for use in the missile's *boost phase*, a beam fired from the ground cannot bend with the curvature of the earth; therefore, the lasers would be carried aboard a fleet of satellites in low orbit. The chemical laser takes up to 10 seconds to destroy the missile, but it is estimated that at least 100 of these lasers must be in orbit at all times.

Excimer Lasers are much more intense laser beams requiring only one second to destroy a missile. Because this laser device is too heavy to lift off the ground, its laser would have to be fired into space from a mountaintop where it would be reflected off a mirror toward its target.

Particle Beams are streams of subatomic particles—electrons, protons and neutrons—accelerated almost to the speed of light. The particle beams would destroy the missile during the *boost phase*. The accelerators, or atom smashers, are currently too big to lift into orbit and cannot be fired from a mountaintop because the particles would be unable to penetrate the atmosphere. The magnetic forces in space also would deflect the beams, making them extremely difficult to aim.

Smart Rocks, or kinetic-energy projectiles approximately 6 × 9 inches in size, travel 6 to 25 miles per second with a range of 1,000 miles using heat sensors to seek out and destroy a missile on impact. They can be carried by ground-based rockets to intercept warheads in their late *mid-course* or *terminal phase;* or fired from a space-based rail gun that would use a strong electric current and its magnetic field to fling the "smart rock" toward the warhead during its *boost* or *mid-course phase.*

Many critics contend that the prospect of success in an anti-ballistic missile defense is unlikely and its pursuit extremely costly because space-based weapons could be readily countered by relatively cheap devices such as anti-satellite weapons.

The Soviet Union has tested, with indifferent success, a relatively low-altitude orbiting interceptor. The United States has conducted tests involving a more sophisticated system capable of destroying satellites at higher altitudes. This consists of a miniature homing device carried and launched by an F-15 fighter airplane.

Ironically, any breakthrough in achieving a space-based system to destroy ballistic missiles would also increase the vulnerability of the space-based system itself. Anti-satellite systems and space-based strategic defensive systems are the subject of one of the three sets of strategic arms talks taking place in Geneva.

Moreover, the Strategic Defense Initiative, or Star Wars space-based system, could not defend against Soviet bombers or ground-hugging cruise missiles; and if pursued to the testing stage, this effort would require the abrogation of the ABM Treaty.

Source of Information: *U.S. Arms Control and Disarmament Agency and Arms Control Association*

Other Weapons of Mass Destruction: Chemical and Biological Weapons

As a result of the abhorrent devastation caused by the use of chemical weapons in World War I, 105 nations signed the Geneva Protocol of 1925 to ban the use in war of asphyxiating, poisonous, or other gases, and of biological weapons of warfare. The production and stockpiling of these lethal weapons, however, were not prohibited.

Since the 1960s, the Conference on Disarmament and its predecessors have been working in Geneva to negotiate global bans on chemical and biological weapons. The Biological and Toxin Weapons Convention was completed in 1972 and prohibited the development, production, and stockpiling of biological and toxin weapons. Negotiations on chemical disarmament are on-going.

The subject of chemical and biological weapons takes on a renewed sense of urgency in light of the use of this type of warfare in the Iran-Iraq conflict of the 1980s and the suspicions that some Third World nations may have obtained this awesome capability.

The use of chemical weapons by Iraq against the Kurds and against ill-equipped Iranian military personnel reportedly produced heavy casualties and is thought to have been a contributing factor to the ceasefire move by Iran. Syria and Libya, among the many others, are also reported to be producing and stockpiling chemical weapons.

These weapons have been characterized as the smaller nations' alternative to a nuclear arsenal—a "poor man's atom bomb."

The Nixon administration announced in 1969 its decision to stop producing chemical weapons. In 1981, 1982, and 1983, Congress refused to end the U.S. moratorium on producing new chemical weapons; however, Congress changed its view and voted in 1987 to authorize some production.

The United States and the Soviet Union possess by far the world's largest chemical arsenals. The U.S. stockpile is estimated to include some 30,000 tons of chemical agents including both nerve agents and mustard gas.

In 1987, the United States began producing new 155mm artillery *"binary"* nerve gas shells as well as chemical warheads for the *Multiple*

Launch Rocket System (MLRS). The new weapon is called "binary" because it consists of two chemicals that only become lethal when mixed during use.

As new chemical weapons are produced, older weapons are being destroyed. The United States has agreed to withdraw its current European chemical stockpile from the Federal Republic of Germany by 1992. In fact, in July 1990, the United States announced a halt in its production of binary weapons.

The Soviet Union announced at the end of 1987 that its stockpiles of chemical weapons do not exceed 50,000 tons of poison substances. Although intelligence evidence on the size of the Soviet stockpile is reportedly highly fragmentary, the Soviet Union announced that it had ceased production of chemical weapons in 1987 and would begin dismantling some of its current stockpile by the end of 1989 or when the chemical dismantlement complex at Chapeyevsk is completed.

Negotiations toward a global ban on all chemical weapons are ongoing in the 40-nation Conference on Disarmament in Geneva, and the 1989 Paris Conference called for completion of such a Chemical Weapons Convention as "urgent." The convention would ban all development, possession, production, acquisition, transfer, and use of chemical weapons. All existing chemical weapons would be destroyed by the year 2000 under international inspection and production facilities would be eliminated.

The Soviets have accepted the essence of the U.S. position on verification of a chemical weapons ban including extensive on-site inspections.

The 1972 Biological and Toxin Weapons Convention bans both the use and possession of biological and toxin weapons, except in small amounts for defensive research. Toxins are highly poisonous chemicals produced by living organisms. They are covered by the convention even if synthesized artificially.

The United States charges that the Soviet Union has violated the agreement by the alleged transfer of toxin weapons to the Vietnamese for use in Southeast Asia—the so-called *yellow rain;* by the alleged use of toxin weapons in Afghanistan; and by the outbreak of *anthrax* in the Soviet city of Sverdlovsk in 1979, allegedly due to an accident at a facility suspected of carrying out prohibited biological warfare activities. The Soviet Union has adamantly denied all of the charges.

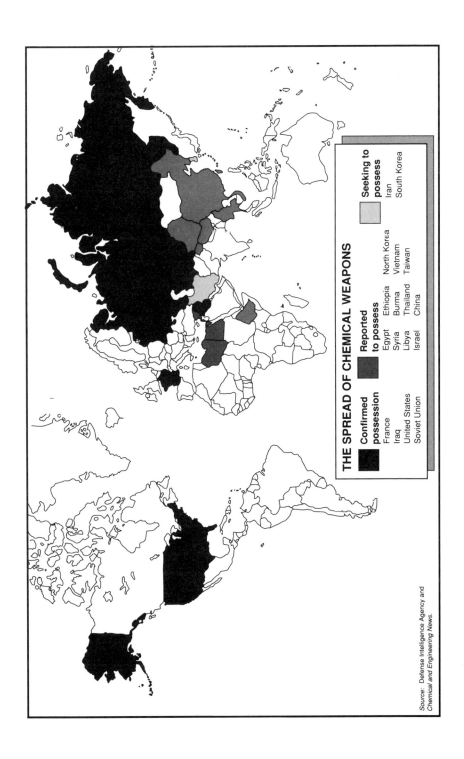

THE SPREAD OF CHEMICAL WEAPONS

Confirmed possession
France
Iraq
United States
Soviet Union

Reported to possess
Egypt   Ethiopia
Syria   Burma
Libya   Thailand
Israel   China
North Korea
Vietnam
Taiwan

Seeking to possess
Iran
South Korea

Source: Defense Intelligence Agency and Chemical and Engineering News.

Types of Chemical Weapons

Chemical agents of warfare are chemical substances—whether gaseous, liquid, or solid—employed because of their direct toxic effects on man, animals, and plants.

The chemical weapons in current stockpiles include:

Nerve agents—colorless, odorless, tasteless chemicals of the same family as insecticides that poison the nervous system and disrupt vital body functions. They constitute the most modern war chemicals known. They kill quickly and are more potent than are any other chemical agents with the exception of toxins.

Blister agents—oily liquids that burn and blister the skin within hours after exposure and have general toxic effects. Mustard gas is an example. Blister agents caused more casualties in World War I than any other chemical agent.

Choking agents—highly volatile liquids that, when breathed as gases, irritate and severely injure the lungs, causing death from choking. They are of much lower potency than the nerve agents.

Blood agents—intended to enter the body through the respiratory tract, causing death by interfering with the utilization of oxygen by the tissues. They, too, are much less toxic than nerve agents.

Toxins—biologically produced chemical substances that are very highly toxic and may act by ingestion or inhalation.

Tear gases—sensory irritants that cause a temporary flow of tears, irritation of the skin and respiratory tract and, occasionally, nausea and vomiting. They have been widely used as riot-control agents as well as in war.

Psycho-chemicals—drug-like chemicals intended to cause temporary mental disturbances.

Herbicides (defoliants such as Agent Orange)—agricultural chemicals that poison or dessicate the leaves of plants, causing the plants to lose their leaves and die.

Binary chemical weapons—include two relatively harmless chemicals stored separately but when mixed become highly toxic after the weapons are launched.

Types of Biological Weapons

Biological or bacteriological agents of warfare are living organisms, whatever their nature, or infective material derived from them that are intended to cause disease or death in man, animals, or plants, and depend for their effects on their ability to multiply in the person, animal, or plant attacked. Some of the various living organisms used as weapons are:

Viruses, which are the smallest forms of life, must be grown on living tissue cultures, fertile eggs, and so on. Genetic manipulation of the virus or chemical manipulation of its nucleic acid can be used to achieve greater capability of destruction.

Rickettsiae also grow only in living tissue; however, research into the genetics has been less intense than into that of viruses and bacteria.

Bacteria are larger than viruses and can be easily grown on a large scale. Although disease-producing bacteria are susceptible to antibiotic drugs, antibiotic-resistance can be obtained through genetic manipulation.

Fungi produce a number of diseases in man, but few species of fungi appear to have potential in biological warfare.

Protozoa, one-celled organisms, cause several human diseases including malaria.

Although there are some similarities between **chemical and biological agents,** such as the means of delivery by discharge into the atmosphere, there are certain important areas of differences such as:

Potential Toxicity. Chemical warfare agents are far less potent than are biological agents. Because biological agents are living organisms, they can multiply and inflict casualties over a much more extensive area than could chemical weapons.

Speed of Action. Chemical agents produce their injurious effects in man, animals, or plants more rapidly than do biological agents. Highly toxic gases may do its work in minutes or seconds; blister agents in a few hours; chemicals against crops in a few days. Biological agents, however, must multiply in the body of the victim before disease or injury supervenes. This process can be as short as one or two days or as long as a few weeks.

Duration of Effect. The effects of *chemical agents* that do not kill quickly do not last long, except in the case of some agents such as mustard gas that may continue for weeks, months, or longer. *Biological agents* that are not quickly lethal cause illnesses lasting days or even weeks and involve periods of prolonged convalescence.

Specificity. *Biological agents*, in general, have a much greater degree of specificity in their intended targets than do *chemical agents*.

Controllability. Because they afflict living organisms, *biological agents* can be carried by man, animals or birds to localities far from the area originally attacked. This kind of spread does not apply to *chemical agents*, but control of chemical contamination could prove very difficult. For example, should large quantities of chemical agents penetrate the soil and reach underground waters or should they contaminate reservoirs, the agents could spread hundreds of miles from the area of attack.

Residual Effects. In some circumstances, herbicides, defoliants, and some other *chemical agents* might linger for months, stunting the growth of surviving or subsequent plant life, and could influence soil structure. Because of their ability to cause disease in man, animals, and plants that could lead to widespread epidemics, *biological agents* pose potentially greater risks.

Source of Information: *A United Nations Report*

Verification

As used in the vocabulary of arms control, **verification** means the process of determining whether there has been compliance with the provisions of arms control treaties and agreements. It is the attempt to make sure, through the application of modern intelligence techniques, that activities prohibited by a treaty are in fact not taking place.

Monitoring—the collection of intelligence data—is the initial stage in the verification process. When the data are obtained, they must be evaluated with a view to the provisions of a particular agreement, and evidence must be assembled for possible noncompliance. The evidence as a whole serves as the basis for deciding whether an issue of violation is involved. Since data with respect to compliance may be subject to differing interpretations, judgment and decision at the political level is frequently required.

Once nuclear weapons became a part of national arsenals, their unprecedented destructive power made it imperative to seek international agreement on the limitation and reduction of arms. Yet the potential for concealment of nuclear devices, together with the speed with which nuclear weapons can reach their targets, and the difficulty of defense in a period of rapid development of missile technology, make effective verification of agreements both difficult and necessary.

In 1946, the **Baruch Plan**, the first American proposal for the control of nuclear weapons presented to the United Nations, called for an international agency to own and supervise the production of nuclear materials solely for peaceful purposes. It proposed a continuing system of inspection to guard against the illicit production and stockpiling of nuclear weapons. The Soviet government objected to the extent of its provisions on inspection and control, and Soviet counterproposals were regarded by the United States and other nations as wholly inadequate for verification purposes.

By 1955, the United States and the Soviet Union had come to acknowledge that any accounting of nuclear weapons and materials already produced would be extremely difficult to verify. This, along with the inability to determine the extent of proliferation of such weapons to other countries, meant that complete elimination of such weapons was not a practicable goal for the foreseeable future. Accordingly, attention began to focus on the possibilities of limitation and reduction with measures that would facilitate them such as a ban on nuclear testing and steps to avert the danger of surprise attack.

At a conference in Geneva that same year, President Eisenhower proposed an **Open Skies Plan** that called for inspection of United States and Soviet territory by aircraft of the other side as a warning system against surprise attack. The Soviet Union rejected this plan. (This proposal was renewed by President Bush in a speech in the spring of 1989.) However, the concept of this type of inspection, on a multilateral basis rather than under the auspices of an international body, was put into practical use in the 18-nation **Antarctic Treaty of 1959.** Under the terms of this treaty, all parties, including the Soviet Union, agreed to open their installations on that continent to inspection by any of the other signatory nations.

In 1958, a meeting in Geneva of technical experts from the West and the Soviet bloc concluded that a complete ban on nuclear testing could be adequately verified by the existing techniques of seismic monitoring with on-site inspections to clear up ambiguous cases. It also recommended establishing a network of monitoring posts, under international authority, in the territory of the nuclear powers and in conveniently situated third countries.

Later that year, experts met in Geneva to consider possible techniques for monitoring military deployments in order to detect preparations of surprise attack. At this conference, the Soviet Union proposed a warning system involving aerial reconnaissance as well as ground observation posts along the East-West border. Technical possibilities of photographic and radar reconnaissance by orbiting space satellites were first being explored at this time.

In the following years, efforts to negotiate a comprehensive test ban involving on-site inspections and an international system of verification proved unsuccessful. Concerns about the adequacy of techniques for monitoring underground tests at long range and opposition from proponents of further nuclear weapons development prevented negotiations of a comprehensive ban.

In September 1961, the United States and Great Britain proposed a ban on atmospheric nuclear tests that would be monitored solely by "existing means of detection." These would include photographic, radar, and electronic surveillance capabilities; seismic instrumentation that detects the location and magnitude of underground nuclear explosions; air sampling systems of high sensitivity; and advanced techniques for the analysis and evaluation of the data collected. An agreement was eventually reached on a ban on nuclear testing in the atmosphere, under water, and in outer space. The **Limited Test Ban Treaty of 1963,** which relied solely on **national technical means** of verification for monitoring compliance, marked an important step in the history of arms control.

It was recognized, however, that verification of strategic weapons limitations would present greater difficulties and involve greater uncertainties than verification of the Limited Test Ban Treaty. In 1988, the United States and the Soviet Union decided to pursue the possibilities of an agreement on strategic nuclear weapons by also relying on **national technical means.**

In 1972, the SALT I agreements were concluded. Both the **Anti-Ballistic Missile Treaty** (ABM Treaty) and the **Interim Agreement on Strategic Offensive Arms** explicitly provided for verification by **national technical means** at each party's disposal to assure compliance. Each party also agreed not to interfere with the means of verification of the other, and each party agreed not to use deliberate concealment measures that impede verification.

In addition to these provisions, the **Standing Consultative Commission (SCC)** was established as a joint U.S.-U.S.S.R. body charged with promoting implementation of the objectives and provisions of the ABM Treaty and the Interim Agreement as well as the Agreement on Measures to Reduce the Risk of Outbreak of Nuclear War, which was negotiated during SALT I and entered into force on September 30, 1971.

Generally, the commission is responsible for considering questions of compliance with obligations assumed by the U.S. and the U.S.S.R. under the agreements covered; for reconciling any misunderstandings or uncertainties arising in the performance of those obligations; and for considering proposals for increasing the viability of those agreements. The regulations that govern the SCC's internal operation provide that the proceedings of the commission shall be private. This has facilitated the direct and frank exchanges concerning strategic weapons systems and other matters related to SALT agreement implementation that are necessary for the SCC to carry out effectively its assigned responsibilities. The commission operates under instructions and guidance from the highest levels of government. It is clearly understood that each SCC Commissioner keeps his government fully informed in accordance with the pertinent procedures and process of that government.

In November 1972, the second phase of the SALT Talks, aimed at achieving a more comprehensive agreement on strategic offensive arms to replace the Interim Agreement, began and culminated with the signing of the **SALT II Treaty** in June 1979. This treaty covered the systems to be limited, the means of establishing equality in strategic nuclear forces, and specific quantitative and qualitative limits. Adequate verification was a key objective of the SALT process and an essential feature of SALT II.

For each provision and the agreement as a whole, advocates and opponents of SALT debated whether compliance with the limits could be determined to the extent necessary to safeguard our security. Could we identify a treaty violation, if it occurred on a scale large enough to pose a significant military risk, in time to make an appropriate response? Meeting this test is what is meant by the term **adequate verification.** In 1979, the Secretary of Defense, the Secretary of State, and the Chairman of the Joint Chiefs of Staff all testified that compliance with the provisions of the SALT II Treaty was adequately verifiable.

There have been disputes as to whether the Soviets have complied with the SALT accords. During the Nixon, Ford, and Carter administrations, every U.S. concern raised at the SCC was resolved to the satisfaction of these Presidents—either the practices in question stopped, or they were clarified in a way that alleviated U.S. concerns.

Unquestionably, it became harder to resolve SALT compliance questions after 1979. U.S.-Soviet relations steadily worsened, and SALT II compliance questions were aggravated by the U.S. failure to ratify the SALT II Treaty. The term of that Treaty, moreover, extended only through 1985. ABM compliance issues were complicated by President Reagan's proposal to develop a space-based defense against ballistic nuclear missiles, testing of which would be prohibited by the ABM Treaty.

With the inauguration of the Reagan administration in 1981, the U.S. approach to compliance problems changed considerably. President Reagan and other officials in his administration had long maintained that the Soviets frequently violated SALT and other arms control treaties. In office, they were less inclined than previous administrations to use the SCC to settle disagreements quietly.

Beginning in 1984, the U.S. government issued annual reports detailing alleged Soviet violations of arms control agreements. The Soviet Union responded with accusations of its own against the United States. Many independent experts were inclined to believe that both sets of charges were greatly exaggerated, and that both superpowers were in fact meeting their treaty obligations reasonably well. However, the public airing of accusations made it harder to settle these disagreements.

In 1986, the Reagan administration announced that the United States would no longer be bound by the SALT I Interim Agreement or SALT II. As a result, the SCC's jurisdiction only included the ABM Treaty.

When Mikhail Gorbachev became General Secretary of the Soviet Communist Party in 1985, the Soviet attitude toward verification problems began to change. Gorbachev instituted a policy of **glasnost,** or *openness*, which allowed a freer flow of information within the USSR. At the same time, the Soviets—who had typically opposed having foreign inspectors on their territory—became less secretive and closed in discussing military questions.

The biggest breakthrough came with the signing of the **INF Treaty** in 1987. The Soviet Union agreed to extensive on-site inspections, including visits to all the missile bases mentioned in the treaty, observation of missile destruction, and the right to "challenge" inspections if either side suspects violations. In addition, for thirteen years, Soviet inspectors can monitor everything entering and leaving an American missile plant in Utah, while American soldiers watch a similar factory in Russia.

The strict verification provisions of the INF Treaty meant a great deal to the Reagan administration. Entering office as a sharp critic of Soviet performance in arms control, President Reagan could reasonably claim that he had negotiated an arms reduction treaty with tough inspection requirements that would make cheating more difficult than ever before.

In the late 1980s, the Soviets took other steps to indicate that they did not want verification concerns to get in the way of arms control progress. For example, it was apparent that a certain large Soviet radar, near *Krasnoyarsk*, Siberia, violated an important clause in the ABM Treaty. In 1987, the Soviet government invited a team of U.S. congressmen and experts to visit the radar site. The American inspection showed that the radar was far from completion and that construction had stopped, as the Soviets had claimed.

The superpowers also made some progress on the issue of nuclear testing. Though two treaties had been signed in the 1970s limiting the size of permitted nuclear explosions, the United States and the Soviet Union had been unable to reach agreement as to how to verify that no cheating was taking place. In an unprecedented move, the Soviets in 1987 allowed a private American group to set up monitoring stations near the Soviet nuclear testing grounds, thus showing they were now open to new inspection ideas. The next year, the U.S. and Soviet governments each observed a nuclear explosion on each other's territory, and further progress on nuclear testing seemed possible.

As the United States and the Soviet Union negotiated their next major nuclear arms treaty—the Strategic Arms Reduction Treaty (START)—the question of verification surfaced once again. The American negotiators were facing a complex problem. In the past, when the Soviets were very secretive and opposed to all inspections, the question for the United States has been, "How can we verify that the Soviets aren't cheating?" Now that the Soviet Union has accepted extensive on-site inspection, the United States in turn had to allow the Soviets to inspect the U.S. laboratories and missile plants. The question now is, "How much sensitive information is the United States willing to give up in order to gain access to similar Soviet data?"

The dilemma continues. . . .

Source of Information: "Verification: The Critical Elements of Arms Control,"
U.S. Arms Control and Disarmament Agency
"SALT ONE: Compliance,"-"SALT TWO: Verification,"
U.S. Department of State "Annual Reports,"
U.S. Arms Control and Disarmament Agency

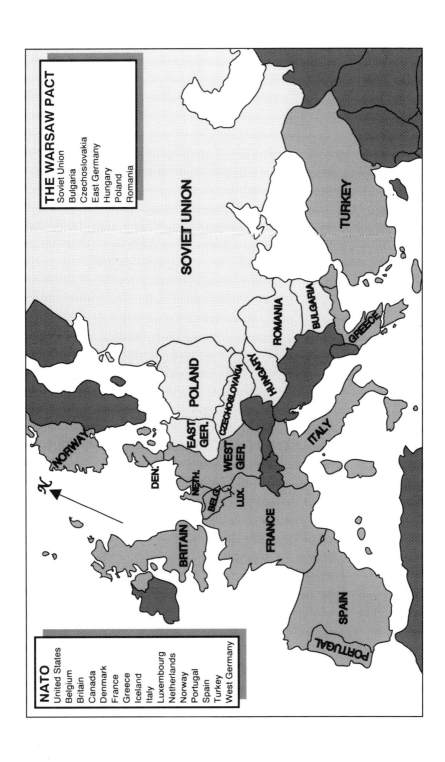

THE WARSAW PACT
Soviet Union
Bulgaria
Czechoslovakia
East Germany
Hungary
Poland
Romania

NATO
United States
Belgium
Britain
Canada
Denmark
France
Greece
Iceland
Italy
Luxembourg
Netherlands
Norway
Portugal
Spain
Turkey
West Germany

SOVIET UNION

POLAND

EAST GER.

CZECHOSLOVAKIA

HUNGARY

ROMANIA

BULGARIA

TURKEY

GREECE

ITALY

WEST GER.

DEN.

NETH.

BELG.

LUX.

FRANCE

BRITAIN

NORWAY

SPAIN

PORTUGAL

Conventional Forces in Europe

		NATO	WARSAW PACT
Personnel		2,213,592	3,090,000
Tanks		23,585	55,848
Combat Aircraft		6,180	11,088
Antitank Weapons		20,940	44,200
Artillery		18,504	49,102
Helicopters		2,599	3,700
Armored Combat Vehicles		30,084	71,300

Source of information: "Conventional Forces in Europe: The Facts," *NATO* (1988).
Institute for Defense & Disarmament Studies, Briefing Paper 1, 1990.
I.D.D.S., Briefing Paper 2, 1990.
Centerpiece of CFE Agreement, 1990.

Conventional Forces

At the NATO summit in May 1989, the Bush administration, under pressure from West Germany and other European allies, agreed to postpone any decision on modernization of shorter-range nuclear missiles in Europe until negotiations reducing the conventional forces could be evaluated. *Conventional forces* or *nonnuclear forces* include *artillery, tanks, armored combat vehicles, combat aircraft and helicopters, and manpower* stationed throughout Europe under the auspices of NATO and the Warsaw Pact.

Beginning in 1974, talks on *Mutual and Balanced Force Reductions (MBFR)* have been held in Vienna. The two alliances failed to agree even on the size of each other's forces in Europe, let alone how to reduce them significantly.

Questions are being raised as to what the numbers mean in terms of which side would be likely to win a non-nuclear European war and what methods are used to assess superiority beyond mere numbers. If negotiations for reducing shorter-range nuclear missiles were to be undertaken, would the U.S. allies in Europe be left vulnerable to the threat of attack from superior Soviet conventional forces?

It has been argued that the statistics taken by themselves do not necessarily prove that the Soviet-led forces would prevail in a conventional war.

There is little doubt that the Warsaw Pact is numerically superior to NATO in front-line ground forces. However, the contention that the Warsaw Pact is superior to NATO in other categories of conventional land-based weaponry deployed in Europe remains questionable. The quality of equipment, the readiness for war—i.e., the mobilization and resupply time—the ability to fight over a long period, alliance loyalty, and other factors all help determine who might possess the military advantage.

Measuring quantity against quality complicates any assessment of the East-West military balance. Some argue that the substantial Warsaw Pact advantage in number of battle tanks is offset by the obsolescence of many of the tanks and by NATO's sophisticated antitank defenses.

Others, however, counter that the Soviets are modernizing their tank fleet and are quickly catching up with the West in antitank technology. The balance is far more complex than is usually portrayed.

A congressional report concludes that the Warsaw Pact forces are superior in six categories including positioning of forces, functioning under a single command, and mobilizing quickly for war. On the other hand, NATO is superior in five categories and roughly equal in two categories.

A typical calculation of 55,800 Warsaw Pact tanks to NATO's 23,500 ignores the fact that half of the Pact tanks are models designed before 1965. Moreover, in the central region of Europe, which is thought likely to be the initial East-West battleground in the event of a conflict, the Warsaw Pact has 18,000 tanks compared with NATO's 12,700. Analysts have suggested NATO's tanks are far superior, thus reducing the apparent difference.

However, to ensure that NATO can adequately defend against a Warsaw Pact attack, the study further reports that major improvements in communications systems and munition stocks are needed. Also needed are standardized weapons for troops from different countries to help avoid confusion on the battlefield.

The two alliances have now scrapped the **MBFR Talks** altogether and opened a new set of talks called **CFE, Conventional Forces in Europe.** The principal reasons for this change are that the new talks will have a different geographical scope—i.e., covering all of Europe from the Atlantic to the Urals rather than just the Central European zone covered in the earlier talks—and will deal with weaponry as well as manpower.

The first major East-West initiative of the Bush administration came after six months of widely criticized Western failure to react to Gorbachev's announcement at the United Nations in December 1988 of a unilateral cut of 500,000 troops in Soviet forces worldwide and substantial reductions of forward-based tanks, artillery, and manpower in Europe.

The United States' proposal covered the following:

- the United States would reduce combat troops in Europe from about 305,000 to 275,000 while the Soviet Union would reduce its European troops from 600,000 to 275,000 troops;

- NATO's tanks to be reduced from 23,500 to 20,000 and those of the Warsaw Pact from 55,000 to 20,000;

- NATO's armored combat vehicles to be scaled down from approximately 30,000 to 28,000 and those of the Warsaw Pact from about 71,000 to 28,000;

- NATO's artillery tubes from 18,500 to 16,500 and those of the Warsaw Pact from 49,000 to 16,500;

- NATO's fixed-wing combat aircraft to be cut back from 6,100 to 4,600 and those of the Warsaw Pact from 11,000 to 4,600; and

- NATO's attack and assault helicopters to be cut from 2,600 to 2,200 and those of the Warsaw Pact from 3,700 to 2,200.

President Bush set 1992–1993 as a target date for implementation of an agreement, not 1997 as proposed by General Secretary Gorbachev.

The dramatic developments in Eastern Europe have rendered this proposal obsolete. Informal agreement has already been reached that the United States and the Soviet Union each will keep no more than 195,000 troops in Central Europe, with an additional 30,000 American troops elsewhere in Europe. Even these figures are probably higher than can be maintained, given political developments and budget pressures.

Authority to Release Nuclear Weapons

Authorization for the use of nuclear weapons comes from the President of the United States as Commander-in-Chief. In the event of his incapacitation, the line of authority runs to the Vice President and then to the Secretary of Defense, not the Secretary of State.

The means by which the President directs the use of nuclear weapons starts with the so-called *Black Bag* or *Football,* usually carried by an Army Lieutenant Colonel who accompanies the President at all times. The attaché case contains *Gold Codes* (a random jumble of letters and numbers, changed daily by the National Security Agency, and simultaneously delivered to nuclear command posts around the world); the options specified in the *Single Integrated Operational Plan (SIOP)* (a plan that accounts for the nuclear weapons of all three branches of the United States military and integrates all the nuclear contingency plans of the regional commands in the Pacific, the Atlantic, and Europe); and the President's decision book containing the instructions for release and execution of the SIOP.

Implementation of the President's decision to release nuclear weapons involves a complex series of steps designed to prevent unauthorized or accidental use.

Under the Constitution of the United States, the Congress has the power to declare war, but as Commander-in-Chief, the President has primary responsibility for the defense of the United States. Recognition of the facts of modern warfare and the existence of nuclear weapons that could strike targets in the United States within minutes led to the enactment of the *War Powers Act* in 1973 giving the President the authority to conduct a war—conventional or nuclear—for 60 days without congressional approval. Within this period, Congress can take action to terminate use of American forces. The President is required, however, to submit a report to Congress explaining his action within 48 hours of committing American forces into combat. As a practical matter, however, the decision to use nuclear weapons resides within the Executive Branch.

The greatest degree of control and direction exists with respect to the use of intercontinental ballistic missiles and strategic bombers under the Strategic Air Command (SAC). The present *National Command and Control System* was created as a result of a conclusion reached in the early 1960s by the Joint Chiefs of Staff who warned Secretary of Defense Robert McNamara that the U.S. early warning and command and control system would not be able to survive a nuclear attack.

The **Command, Control, and Communications** structure (C^3) includes the following:

National Military Command Center (NMCC)—a main operations room located in the Pentagon—is the central facility through which the President would interact with the warning and control system. It has direct communications with all subordinate command centers around the world and has links to the nuclear forces enabling the commanders to deliver Gold Codes directly to missile silos, bomber crews, and submarine commanders.

Alternate Military Command Center (ALMCC)—located deep in a mountain in Pennsylvania (Raven Rock)—is the alternate to the NMCC to be used only in time of nuclear war. Eight miles south is Camp David, which also has an underground emergency operations center that can serve as a nuclear war command post and is linked by a buried cable to the post in Raven Rock.

North American Aerospace Defense Command (NORAD)—buried deep inside the Cheyenne Mountain in Colorado—is the center where indications and warning information from multiple sources are monitored continuously and relayed to other major command centers. NORAD is an Air Force command effectively linked with SAC but serves as a separate organization with the responsibility for air defense against Soviet attack. This organizational structure does not leave decision-making in the hands of any one organization, thus preventing unauthorized or inadvertent use of nuclear weapons.

When Soviet nuclear weapons were carried on bombers rather than missiles, NORAD was created and established as a joint United States–Canada command because the route of Soviet bombers would bring them over Canada. Accordingly, many radars and fighter bases were located in Canada. Because the NORAD weapons were defensive in nature, the NORAD Commander was given a significant delegation of authority to use them, subject to severe restrictions and specific conditions of attack. The weapons he might release would not be of a type that could strike Soviet targets.

Strategic Air Command (SAC)—located in an underground bunker at Offutt Air Force Base in Omaha—has the most effective control with respect to intercontinental ballistic missiles and strategic bomber forces. The SAC Commander has the authority to launch a bomber force to prevent its destruction on the ground by attacking missiles. Once airborne, they hold position awaiting orders from SAC as to whether to proceed or return depending on the threat of the incoming attack, which is determined by NORAD. On the SAC Commander's desk is an array of seven different colored telephones with permanently open lines to SAC operations worldwide and to the National Command Authority in Washington.

> ***Land-Based Missiles.*** On a shelf between the two crewmen in a Minuteman missile silo is the ***red box***—an exact replica of those inside the missile submarine command and control center and B-52 cockpits. Secured with two combination locks are the ***validation codes*** that authenticate the "nuclear control order" and two keys for missiles' release. In response to an initial alert command from the SAC controller, an alarm rings inside the capsule and the senior crew member receives an "Emergency Action Message"—an authorized launch instruction from the National Command Authority. The crew commander copies the twelve number and letter code that follows immediately and verifies it with that particular day's launch codes while a hard copy confirmation of the oral message is delivered over a small teletype machine.
>
> Each crew member opens one of the two locks on the red box, removes the sealed "Emergency War Order"—the special instructions for firing the missiles. They also remove their silver firing keys. The launch officers then jointly validate the Emergency Action Message with the launch codes. The crew then waits for the "release message" called the ***Nuclear Control Order.***
>
> Before the crews are able to turn their keys to launch their missile, a second crew, in one of the other four launch control centers, must go through the same procedure to validate the launch command; or they can delay and ultimately prevent a launch if they believe it to be the result of an invalid order. The delay lasts for a few minutes and then is automatically cancelled.

Finally, the two crewmen must turn their keys simultaneously and hold them in position for at least five seconds to launch a missile. During this operation, the lit panels on the crewmen's consoles have progressed through launch sequences beginning with "strategic alert" to "warhead armed" to "launch in progress" and ending with "missiles away." Once the missile is fired, there is no recall.

Submarines. The greater difficulty in communicating with our strategic submarines has always posed the risk of accident. The fact that ballistic missile submarines (SSBNs) must often operate thousands of miles from the National Command Centers and are usually cruising deep under water, has required more extensive delegation of release authority. Efforts have been made to improve communication through underground systems in the American midwest. Moreover, the increased range of the Trident I or C4 submarine-launched ballistic missile has significantly ameliorated the communications difficulty. The submarines can now operate much closer to the coast of the United States. The greater security from possible enemy attack and the shorter distance communications must travel provide greater continuity and effectiveness of communications and control.

The issue of authority to use nuclear weapons is a very difficult one because of conflicting considerations. The desirability of a quick response, in some circumstances, would tend toward delegation and the short-cutting of complex procedures. The momentous and fatal consequences of premature and imprudent use of nuclear weapons, however, tend toward elaborate and time-consuming procedures.

This conflict has characterized debate about the use of tactical or battlefield nuclear weapons and has led to proposals for creation of a nuclear weapons-free corridor in central Europe. Inevitably, compromises have had to be made, and no truly satisfactory system for release and use of nuclear weapons is possible.

Renewed concern about the survivability of the U.S. **Command, Control, and Communications (C³)** led to a decision announced in October 1981 to make further improvements and refinements. The exact nature of these changes is highly classified.

Source of Information: U.S. Department of Defense Publications and
U.S. Congressional Committee Reports

Section IV

- **The Negotiating Process**

- **The SALT Talks**

    ABM Treaty
    Interim Agreement on Offensive Weapons
    SALT II Treaty

- **The START Talks**

- **The INF Talks**

- **Existing Treaties and Agreements**

- **Ongoing Arms Control Negotiations**

- **Violation Concerns of the U.S. and U.S.S.R.**

    Prior to 1980
    After 1980

"The security gained by the United States and its allies through past arms control agreements and the prospects for further restraints on nuclear weapons are being threatened.

"As a result, the United States and the Soviet Union will face a double-barreled arms race where all of us will lose."

> Gerard C. Smith
> Chief SALT I Negotiator
> Nixon Administration

"In previous eras, great powers could continue to arm and consider themselves to be stronger and more secure. As the nuclear arms race developed, both the United States and the Soviet Union recognized that this simple principle no longer necessarily applied. The more each side armed with nuclear weapons, the less secure each might become.

"An unlimited arms race—one without rules—might be so dangerous as to lead to the outbreak of a war which would have no victors."

> Paul C. Warnke
> Chief SALT II Negotiator
> Carter Administration

The Negotiating Process

The negotiating positions of the United States on the subject of limiting and reducing nuclear weapons between it and the Soviet Union are discussed and adopted by the National Security Council (NSC) with the participation of the

President
Vice President
Secretary of State
Secretary of Defense
Chairman of the Joint Chiefs of Staff
Director of the Central Intelligence Agency
Director of the U.S. Arms Control & Disarmament Agency
President's National Security Advisor

Position papers are prepared for NSC consideration by an interagency working group of government officials representing these agencies.

Although our information on Soviet decision-making is incomplete and uncertain, negotiating positions of the Soviet Union are believed to be determined by the twenty-member Politburo, the highest governing group, on the basis of positions developed separately by the relevant agencies. Primarily these agencies are the Ministry of Defense and the Ministry of Foreign Affairs. Any disagreements appear to be resolved at the Politburo level without previous processing by an interagency working group.

The SALT Talks

Strategic arms limitation talks between the United States and the Soviet Union began in 1969 and were conducted—under the acronym **SALT**—during the administrations of three American presidents: Richard Nixon, Gerald Ford, and Jimmy Carter. The purpose of the talks was to promote U.S. national security by reducing the risk of nuclear war through negotiation of mutual limits on strategic nuclear arms.

All three administrations articulated general principles that guided their conduct of negotiations:

- agreements reached should permit the United States to maintain strategic forces at least equal to those of the Soviet Union;

- agreements should maintain and, if possible, enhance the stability of the strategic balance, thereby reducing the likelihood of nuclear war; and

- agreements should be adequately verifiable so that Soviet violations of any significance would be detected and acted upon.

When the United States and the Soviet Union were beginning to build a defensive system—the Anti-Ballistic Missile System (ABM)—each side had growing doubts as to whether, in an initial attack, the system would work well enough to prevent attacking missiles from inflicting enormous damage. Both sides recognized that missile defenses, no matter how sophisticated, could still be outsmarted by offensive improvement and, as a consequence, spur on the arms race. For this reason, the first phase of the SALT process began in 1969.

Under the direction of President Nixon and National Security Advisor Henry Kissinger, the first results of the SALT process were realized in a **SALT I Agreement,** which consisted of two parts—the **ABM Treaty** and the **Interim Agreement**—both concluded in 1972.

Today, there are some who advocate exotic defensive weapons including those based in outer space. But most experts feel that the same problems exist with futuristic weapons as with the ones each superpower worked on when the ABM Treaty was signed. There is no reason to believe that any available or presently foreseeable technology would provide an effective defense against thousands of incoming warheads. Accordingly, the deployment of futuristic weapons would be a destabilizing influence, expensive to deploy, and relatively simple to defeat.

The ABM Treaty

The ABM Treaty, signed in 1972 by the United States and the Soviet Union, was of unlimited duration with joint U.S. and Soviet reviews every five years. The **ABM Treaty** severely limits **defensive systems** designed to intercept and destroy attacking missiles. The Treaty and a Protocol to it limit each side to one ABM installation of not more than 100 missiles and launchers that can be deployed around either an ICBM site or the national capital.

The ABM Treaty also prohibits development, testing, and deployment of sea-based, air-based, space-based, and mobile land-based ABM systems and their component parts. Some research and development for new ABMs is permitted by the Treaty but on a very limited scale.

In 1977, the United States and the Soviet Union conducted a review of the ABM Treaty and both sides agreed that the Treaty had operated effectively, continued to serve the interests of both sides, and needed no amendments. The second review was held in 1982, and both countries came to similar conclusions.

The Interim Agreement on Offensive Weapons

The second half of the SALT I accords was an **Interim Agreement on Offensive Weapons.** While the agreement was not a complete freeze on strategic nuclear weapons because it allowed certain replacements and substitutes, it called for a halt to construction of new ICBM silos and placed ceilings on various categories of weapon launchers.

Under the Interim Agreement, both sides were permitted to expand their sea-based missile forces only if they dismantled an equal number of older land- or sea-based missile launchers. Both countries agreed to follow up the Interim Agreement with active negotiations for more comprehensive limitations in the arms race. Thus the Interim Agreement was a holding action to complement the ABM Treaty, to limit competition in **offensive weapons**, and to provide a framework for further negotiations.

Unfortunately, the Interim Agreement counted and limited only the launchers of strategic weapons, not the number of warheads on them. Because multiple independently-targetable reentry vehicles (MIRVs) were not limited, both sides began to multiply the destructive power of their existing missiles, despite the freeze on launchers. The U.S. began to deploy MIRVs in 1970; the Soviet Union began in 1975.

One of the negotiating options under a review by the United States government in late 1969 and 1970 was a ban on MIRV testing. The idea was that if neither side flight-tested its missiles with MIRVs, neither could have confidence that MIRVs would work as designed. During this time, the Soviet Union was rapidly deploying new land-based and sea-based missiles; the United States was not. Key officials in Congress and in the Nixon White House felt that MIRVs were necessary to offset the buildup of Soviet missiles. The U.S. had already begun to test MIRVs; the Soviets had not. So these individuals did not wish to give up a clear U.S. advantage.

One concern that was raised at the time was how a MIRV ban could be verified. Officials within the U.S. Arms Control and Disarmament Agency, the Department of State, and the Central Intelligence Agency believed verification by remote devices such as photo-reconnaissance satellites, ground-based radars, and collection of radio transmissions—collectively known as **National Technical Means**—would be adequate. President Nixon and National Security Advisor Kissinger disagreed, as did Pentagon officials. The U.S. proposed that a ban on MIRVs be linked to "on-site inspection" at Soviet missile bases. The Soviets rejected on-site inspection. They proposed that MIRVs be flight-tested but not deployed. But once flight-tested, there was no way to prove that MIRVs were not placed atop missiles except by on-site inspection.

In other words, neither side was sufficiently concerned about MIRVs in the SALT I negotiations to ban or severely limit them.

As a result, within eight years, the Soviets MIRVed about half of their land-based missiles. When these missiles became increasingly accurate, in theory, they placed U.S. land-based missiles at risk—the so-called **window of vulnerability.**

Because the Interim Agreement was intended to be just what its name indicates, it was presented to Congress as an Executive Agreement, not as a treaty. Of five years' duration, the Agreement entered into force on October 3, 1972, and expired on October 3, 1977. At that time, the United States and the Soviet Union separately stated that they did not plan to take any action inconsistent with the provisions of the Interim Agreement pending conclusion of the SALT II negotiations.

SALT II Treaty

Early discussion between the United States and the Soviet Union on a **SALT II Treaty** began in November 1972. It covered a variety of issues including the systems to be limited, the means of establishing equality in strategic nuclear forces, and specific quantitative and qualitative limits. The positions of the two sides differed widely on many of these questions, and only limited progress was made in the first two years.

A major breakthrough occurred in November 1974 at the Vladivostok meeting between President Gerald Ford and the Soviet leader Leonid Brezhnev. They agreed on basic guidelines for a SALT II agreement and a common ceiling of 2400 strategic weapon launchers per side of which no more than 1320 could be launchers of MIRVed missiles.

Finally, after almost five more years of difficult negotiations, an agreement was reached that accommodated both the Soviet desire to retain the Vladivostok framework for an agreement and the U.S. desire for more comprehensive limitations.

The SALT II Agreement consists of three parts:

- a **Treaty** that would incorporate and reduce the limits of the Vladivostok accord and that would be in force through 1985;

- a **Protocol** that would prohibit through 1981 the deployment of weapons about which both sides had the greatest difficulty in agreeing—ground-launched and sea-launched cruise missiles and mobile ICBMS; and

- a **Joint Statement of Principles**—an agreed set of guidelines for further negotiations.

The SALT II Treaty, the most detailed and far-reaching agreement in the history of nuclear arms control, was to be in effect through December 1985. It provided for a limit of 2250 (down from 2400 at Vladivostok) on the total number of strategic nuclear delivery vehicles, namely:

ICBMs   InterContinental Ballistic Missiles

SLBMs   Submarine-Launched Ballistic Missiles

Heavy Bombers, including those carrying long-range
                    cruise missiles

Within the total ceiling of 2250, each side has the right to determine the number of weapons it prefers to have within each category, but with limitations.

The agreement also provides for:

- a ban on construction of additional fixed ICBM launchers and on the modifications each side can make to existing ICBMs;

- a ban on flight-testing or deployment of new types of ICBMs, except for one new land-based missile with a limit of 10 warheads;

- a ban on increasing the number of warheads on existing types of land-based ICBMs and a limit of 14 warheads on sea-based SLBMs;

- a limit on the average number of long-range cruise missiles to 28 on each side's bomber force and a limit of 20 on existing heavy bombers (B-52s);

- a ban on the production, testing, and deployment of the Soviet SS-16 missile designed for mobile launchers, including a ban on the production of that missile's components; and

- an exchange of data on the systems included in the various SALT-limited categories in order to establish an agreed base to measure reductions.

The **SALT II Treaty** was completed and signed by President Carter and President Brezhnev in Vienna on June 18, 1979. The Treaty has not been ratified by the U.S. Senate but is still tacitly honored by both sides.

The START Talks

The Strategic Arms Reduction Talks (START)—formerly known as SALT—are a continuation of the negotiations between the United States and the Soviet Union on *strategic (long-range) nuclear weapons.*

While the SALT Treaty put ceilings on the number of weapon delivery systems, the current outline of a START treaty would reduce the U.S. and U.S.S.R. nuclear weapons arsenals by about 30 to 35 percent, with greater cuts in ballistic missiles. Both the United States and the Soviet Union believe that these sharp reductions would lower the risk of a nuclear conflict.

The START Treaty would include areas *not* included in the SALT Treaty—i.e., the limiting of nuclear warheads, rather than simply delivery systems, and sublimits on the number of warheads on ballistic missiles.

One of the major points still unresolved is the kind of procedures for verifying specific weapons systems. Mobile ICBMs pose additional verification problems since this type of ICBM can easily be concealed and difficult to count. The United States has proposed a ban of mobile ICBMs unless acceptable procedures for verification can be negotiated. However, development is proceeding both on the mobile Midgetman and a rail-based MX.

SLCMs (submarine-launched cruise missiles) are difficult to verify because of their small size and multiplicity of launching platforms. Therefore, the United States and the Soviet Union have agreed that SLCMs would not be included under the launcher and warhead ceilings. Both sides, however, continue to explore possibilities for limiting or eliminating nuclear SLCMs.

Another point of disagreement involves the sublimits within the ballistic missile warhead ceiling. The United States favors a limit of 3300 on ICBM warheads, the strongest part of the Soviet Union's triad. The Soviet Union insists upon an equivalent ceiling on SLBMs, the mainstay of the American nuclear triad.

In addition, the testing of space-based missile defenses, such as the Strategic Defense Initiative (SDI) proposed by President Reagan, remains a controversial issue. The Soviet Union claims that testing of space-based ABM systems would violate the 1972 Anti-Ballistic Missile (ABM) Treaty and for some time refused to sign a START Treaty until this question was resolved. The United States argues that testing of new space-based strategic defense technologies would not violate the ABM Treaty but that the Soviet Union's Krasnoyarsk radar does violate the terms of the treaty. The Krasnoyarsk problem has been resolved by Soviet agreement to dismantle it, and the Soviet Union no longer insists on resolution of the SDI issue by treaty provisions.

Critics of START are fearful that the large reductions in strategic arms would weaken NATO's chief means of deterrence—the threat of a U.S. strategic nuclear response. The alleged conventional superiority of the Soviet Union is also seen as a very real danger to Western Europe, and it has been suggested by some that START should be linked to reductions in conventional forces. On the other hand, supporters of a START Treaty claim that it improves stability because it limits the number of warheads the Soviets have available to strike ICBMs, submarines, and bombers.

Points of the Treaty on which both sides have already agreed are:

- 1600 strategic launchers—ICBMs, SLBMs, Heavy Bombers—and
- 6000 warheads.

The sublimits within these ceilings call for:

- only 4900 of the 6000 warheads may be on ICBMs and SLBMs;
- 154 heavy ICBMs can carry 10 warheads each (the Soviet Union now has 308; the United States has none);
- limitations on the throw-weight of ICBMs and SLBMs; and
- bombs and short-range missiles on heavy bombers are to be calculated as one warhead per bomber regardless of the number actually carried on board.

The INF Talks

The talks on *Intermediate Nuclear Forces (INF)*—those forces capable of striking the Soviet Union from Europe or vice versa— presented very complicated issues.

In the late 1940s, as an alternative to the high cost of maintaining sizeable conventional forces in Europe, nuclear weapons were placed on bombers stationed in Great Britain as part of NATO's strategy of massive retaliation in the event of an attack by the Soviet Union.

In the early 1950s, the United States began to deploy tactical nuclear weapons in Europe for use in the event of an invasion by Warsaw Pact conventional forces. By the end of the decade, the Soviet Union had acquired its own theater nuclear weapons and deployed two types of medium-range missiles—the SS-4 and SS-5—in the European part of the Soviet Union.

In the mid-1960s, the United States wanted to place more emphasis on conventional military forces while European governments wanted to continue to rely on nuclear weapons because of the high expense and logistics burden of a conventional defense. As a compromise, the Western Europeans agreed to a larger role for conventional forces as long as the United States retained the nuclear option. This was called "flexible response"—conventional forces would be used first, but if an attack could not be contained, then NATO could respond first with tactical and, if deemed necessary, with strategic nuclear weapons.

During this period, Great Britain and France also began developing their own nuclear weapons forces.

Throughout the 1970s, the Soviet theater nuclear weapon modernization program continued. Deployment of the Backfire bomber began in 1974. In 1977, the Soviets also began replacing the aging SS-4s and SS-5s with the SS-20, a mobile missile with accurate MIRVed warheads that could reach all of Western Europe. Some SS-20 missiles were also stationed east of the Ural Mountains, where they could cover Asian targets.

In response to a continuing Soviet buildup in its new Inter-mediate-Range Nuclear Weapons—the SS-20—the NATO Defense Ministries in late 1979 decided to pursue a dual strategy of modernization and arms control. This called for the United States to deploy 108 Pershing II ballistic missiles and 464 ground-launched cruise missiles in Western Europe. At the same time, NATO Ministers expressed the view that an arms control initiative should be undertaken to make the strategic situation between East and West more stable.

The INF negotiations started in late 1981. Establishing the terms of negotiation was especially difficult in the European theater because each country had its own interests and view of the problems involved.

The planned deployment of the Pershing II ballistic missile in West Germany and the cruise missile in Holland, Belgium, Great Britain, Italy, and West Germany, along with the statements by U.S. officials about possible limited nuclear war, fueled a strong anti-nuclear movement in Western Europe as well as an all-out Freeze campaign in the United States that called for a halt to testing and production of all nuclear weapons.

Initially, the Reagan administration proposed that the missiles would not be deployed if the Soviet Union eliminated all their SS-20s with three warheads each plus their SS-4s and SS-5s with one warhead each, a total of 600 missiles with 1200 warheads aimed at Western Europe. This proposal was called the zero-option.

The Soviet Union offered a counterproposal calling for withdrawal of some of their SS-20s from European Russia with the freedom to deploy them against China and U.S. bases in Asia.

Subsequently, the Soviets modified their demands and proposed destruction of some SS-20s, SS-4s, and SS-5s with a freeze on SS-20s aimed at Asian targets. They argued that this proposal would eliminate more warheads than the 572 planned for deployment in Europe by NATO and, therefore, would balance the intermediate-range missiles directed at the Soviet Union by NATO, the British, and the French. Their prime objective was to prevent any European missile deployment by NATO.

The Soviet cuts were not deep enough to satisfy NATO, and the Soviets continued to insist that the United States forego any INF deployment in Europe.

At the end of the initial round of negotiations in Geneva, it became evident that there were four fundamental issues on which the sides differed:

1) • the United States proposed elimination of all American and Soviet intermediate-range nuclear missiles;
    • the Soviet Union sought to block the planned missile deployments by the U.S. but was not willing to give up all of its intermediate-range missiles in return;
2) • the United States' objective was to limit only U.S. and Soviet systems;
    • the Soviet Union insisted on including the British and French forces;
3) • the United States called for global limits on intermediate-range missiles;
    • the Soviet Union called for limits on systems only in Europe or intended for use in Europe;
4) • the United States proposed limitations only on intermediate-range missile systems;
    • the Soviet Union wanted to include nuclear capable aircraft.

During the 1982 negotiations, delegation chiefs Paul Nitze and Yuli Kvitsinsky held private discussions—known as the *"walk in the woods"*—wherein it was proposed that the United States would be prepared to forego deployment of the Pershing IIs and would limit cruise missiles to 300 on 75 launchers if the Soviets reduced their forces to 75 SS-20s for a total of 225 warheads.

The United States government rejected the proposal; the talks reached an impasse; and the American missiles were deployed beginning in December 1983. The Soviets walked out of the talks.

In January 1985, the talks were resumed.

In January 1986, Mikhail Gorbachev proposed the elimination of all SS-20s in exchange for the elimination of American Pershing IIs and cruise missiles stationed in Europe. He did not include in his proposal any limits on the British and French nuclear forces. He also agreed to include a ban on all other missile systems with ranges in excess of 300 miles.

In 1987, the United States and the Soviet Union agreed to on-site inspection verification measures, and the treaty was signed at the Washington Summit in December and ratified by Congress in 1988.

Existing Treaties and Agreements

To prevent the spread of nuclear weapons . . .

1959 Antarctic Treaty—demilitarizes the Antarctic and declares that it shall be used for peaceful purposes.

1967 Outer Space Treaty—prohibits placing nuclear or other weapons of mass destruction in outer space and outlaws the establishment of military bases, installations, and fortifications, the testing of any type of weapons, and the conduct of military maneuvers in outer space.

1967 Treaty of Tlatelolco—prohibits the testing, use, manufacture, production, or acquisition by any means of nuclear weapons in Latin America. Under Protocol II, the nuclear weapon states agree to respect the military denuclearization of Latin America.

1968 Non Proliferation Treaty—prohibits the transfer of nuclear weapons by nuclear weapon states and the acquisition of such weapons by adhering non-nuclear weapon states.

1971 Seabed Treaty—prohibits the placement of nuclear weapons or other weapons of mass destruction on the seabed beyond a 12-mile zone.

To reduce the risk of nuclear war . . . (agreements between the U.S. and U.S.S.R. only)

1963 Hot Line Agreement—establishes a direct communications link between the United States and the Soviet Union for use in time of emergency. A 1971 agreement further improved the communications link.

1971 Nuclear Accidents Agreement—provides for immediate notification by the United States and the Soviet Union of an accidental, unauthorized incident, or a possible detonation of a nuclear weapon.

1973 Agreement on Prevention of Nuclear War—provides that the United States and the Soviet Union will take all actions necessary to prevent the outbreak of nuclear war.

To limit nuclear testing . . .

1963 Limited Test Ban Treaty—bans nuclear weapon tests in the atmosphere, in outer space, and under water.

1974 Threshold Test Ban Treaty*—limits the yield of underground U.S. and Soviet nuclear weapons tests to 150 kilotons.

1976 Peaceful Nuclear Explosions Treaty*—complements the 1974 Threshold Test Ban Treaty by prohibiting any individual underground nuclear explosion for peaceful purposes that has a yield of more than 150 kilotons, or any group explosion with a total yield greater than 1500 kilotons.

To limit nuclear weapons . . . (between the U.S. and U.S.S.R. only)

1972 ABM Treaty (SALT I)—limits the deployment of anti-ballistic missile defenses by the United States and the Soviet Union.

1972 Interim Agreement (SALT I)—freezes the aggregate number of U.S. and Soviet ballistic missile launchers for a five-year period.

1979 SALT II Treaty*—limits numbers of strategic nuclear delivery vehicles, launchers of MIRVed missiles, bombers with long-range cruise missiles, warheads on existing ICBMs, etc. Bans testing or deploying new ICBMs.

1988 INF Treaty—provides for the elimination of intermediate-range nuclear forces in Europe and other missile systems with ranges in excess of 300 miles.

Other . . .

1925 Geneva Protocol—bans the use in war of asphyxiating, poisonous, or other gases and of bacteriological methods of warfare.

1972 Biological Weapons Convention—bans the development, production, and stockpiling of biological and toxin weapons; requires the destruction of stocks.

1975 Conference on Security and Cooperation in Europe (CSCE)—contains a provision on confidence-building measures that provides for notification of major military maneuvers in Europe.

1977 Environmental Modification Convention—prohibits the hostile use of techniques that could produce substantial environmental modifications.

1981 Inhumane Weapons Convention*—bans use of fragmentation bombs not detectable in the human body; bans use against civilians of mines, booby traps, and incendiary weapons; requires record-keeping mines.

*not ratified

Ongoing Arms Control Negotiations

Initiated in 1961
Conference of the Committee on Disarmament (CCD)
the central forum dealing with multilateral arms control to discuss general and complete disarmament.

Initiated in 1979
Committee on Disarmament (CD)
created by the 1978 U.N. Special Session on Disarmament; this replaced the Conference of the Committee on Disarmament above.

Initiated in 1973
Mutual and Balanced Force Reductions (MBFR)
multilateral negotiations seeking to limit NATO and Warsaw Pact forces within a limited geographic region. These talks have been terminated and replaced by the broader talks on Conventional Armed Forces in Europe (CFE).

Initiated in 1978
Comprehensive Test Ban Negotiations (CTB)[1]
talks between the United States, the Soviet Union, and Great Britain that seek to end all nuclear weapon tests.

Initiated in 1982
Strategic Arms Reduction Talks (START)
talks between the United States and the Soviet Union on the limitations of strategic nuclear weapons (name changed from SALT to START).

Initiated in 1989
Conventional Forces in Europe (CFE)
talks between the members of NATO and those of the Warsaw Pact on cutting weapons and personnel in the area from the Atlantic to the Urals.

[1] **The Reagan administration suspended these negotiations.**

Source of Information: "Arms Control and Disarmament Agreements,"
U.S. Arms Control and Disarmament Agency

Violation Concerns
Questions Raised by the United States

Prior to 1980

Launch Control Facilities (Special Purpose Silos)

Under Article I of the 1972 Interim Agreement, **the Parties undertake not to start construction of additional fixed land-based intercontinental ballistic missile (ICBM) launchers.**

In 1973, the United States observed excavations at a number of launch sites in the U.S.S.R. If these had been intended to contain ICBMs, they would have constituted a violation. In response to the United States' concern, the U.S.S.R. stated that the excavations were for launch control purposes. As additional intelligence became available, the United States concluded that the silos were indeed designed to serve a launch control function.

Modern Large Ballistic Missiles (SS-19 Issue)

Under Article II of the Interim Agreement, **conversion of land-based launchers for light ICBMs into land-based launchers for heavy ICBMs is prohibited.**

In 1975 when deployment of the SS-19 began, its size caused the United States some concern. Since the U.S. and the U.S.S.R. had not come to an agreement on a quantitative definition of a "heavy" ICBM that would constrain increases in the size of Soviet "light" ICBMs, this was not a violation of the agreement. The Soviet Union had refused to agree to specifications for new ICBMs and the U.S. statement to that effect was unilateral and not binding on the Soviet Union. However, the U.S. purpose in raising this issue with the U.S.S.R. was to emphasize the importance that the United States attached to the distinction between light and heavy ICBMs. Further discussions of this question in the SCC forum were deferred because it was under active consideration in the SALT II negotiations. Since that time, the U.S. and the U.S.S.R. delegations have agreed on a clear demarcation in terms of missile launch-weight and throw-weight between "light" and "heavy" ICBMs in the text of SALT II.

Soviet Dismantling or Destruction of Replaced ICBM Launchers

Under Article III of the Interim Agreement and the Protocol thereto, **the Soviets had to dismantle 51 replaced launchers by early 1976 in accordance with the agreed procedures developed in the SCC.**

When it became apparent that the Soviets had not completed all the required dismantling actions on time according to SCC procedures, the U.S. decided to raise the question with the Soviets. But before the U.S. could do so, the Soviets had acknowledged in the SCC that the dismantling of 41 older ICBM launchers had not been completed in the required time period and predicted completion by June 1976. It also agreed to the U.S. demand that no more submarines with replacement SLBM launchers begin sea trials prior to such completion. Both conditions were met. Although the U.S. has observed some minor procedural discrepancies at a number of these deactivated launch sites and at others as the replacement process continued, all launchers have been in a condition that satisfied the essential substantive requirements, which are that they cannot be used to launch missiles and cannot be reactivated in a short time.

Concealment Measures

Under Article V of the Interim Agreement and Article XII of the ABM Treaty, **interference with the national technical means of verification and use of deliberate concealment measures that impede verification by national technical means are prohibited.**

In 1974, the extent of concealment activities in the U.S.S.R. increased substantially. None of them prevented U.S. verification of compliance with the provisions of the ABM Treaty or the Interim Agreement, but the concern was that they could impede verification in the future if the pattern of concealment measures was permitted to expand. The United States stated its concern, and in early 1975, careful analysis of intelligence information led to the conclusion that there no longer appeared to be an expanding pattern of concealment activities associated with strategic weapons programs in the U.S.S.R.

Denial of Test Information

Under Article V of the Interim Agreement, **encoding missile-test telemetry that impedes verification is a violation.**

During the SALT II negotiations, it was reported that the Soviets were engaged in encoding missile-test telemetry. If this activity had impeded verification of compliance with agreement provisions, this activity would be considered a violation. Prior to 1981, it was agreed that this was not the case.

Antisatellite Systems

Under Article V of the Interim Agreement and Article XII of the ABM Treaty, **actual use of an ASAT system against U.S. national technical means of verification is prohibited.**

It has been alleged that Soviet development of antisatellite systems is a violation of the obligation not to interfere with national technical means of verification of compliance with SALT provisions. Since development of such systems is not prohibited, and since the U.S. recently has tested an ASAT system, such development does not constitute violation of existing agreements. The actual use of an ASAT system against verification satellites is prohibited, but this has not occurred.

Blinding U.S. Satellites

Under Article V of the Interim Agreement and Article XII of the ABM Treaty, **interference with or deliberate concealment measures that impede verification by national technical means of compliance with provisions of the agreement is prohibited.**

In 1975, information suggested possible Soviet use of something like laser energy to "blind" certain U.S. satellites, an activity inconsistent with the obligations of the Interim Agreement and the ABM Treaty. When it was thoroughly analyzed, it was determined that no questionable Soviet activity was involved and that U.S. monitoring capabilities had not been affected. The analysis indicated that the phenomena had resulted from several large fires caused by breaks along natural gas pipelines in the U.S.S.R.

Concealment at Test Range

Under Article V of the Interim Agreement, **deliberate concealment measures are prohibited.**

In 1977, the U.S. observed the use of a large screen over an ICBM launcher undergoing conversion at a test range in the U.S.S.R. The U.S. expressed the view that the use of a covering over an ICBM silo launcher concealed activities from national technical means of verification and could impede verification of compliance with provisions of the Interim Agreement, specifically, the provision which deals with increases in dimensions of ICBM silo launchers. Although the Soviets took the position that the provisions of the Interim Agreement were not applicable to the activity in question, they subsequently removed the net covering.

Mobile ICBMs

Under the Interim Agreement, *development and testing of a mobile ICBM is not prohibited but a unilateral statement of the U.S. expressed the view that deployment of such systems would be inconsistent with the objectives of the agreement.*

The suspicion that the Soviet SS-20, a mobile intermediate-range ballistic missile system, might have ICBM range capabilities has proven to be inaccurate. It is judged to be capable of reaching the Aleutian Islands and western Alaska from eastern U.S.S.R.; however, it cannot reach the contiguous 48 states from any of its likely deployment areas. Although the range capability of any missile system can be extended by reducing the total weight of its payload or adding another propulsion state, there is no evidence that the SS-20 has been tested with such modifications. The U.S. would be able to detect the necessary intercontinental-range testing of such a modified system.

Soviet ABM Radar on Kamchatka Peninsula

Under Article IV of the ABM Treaty, *only those ABM components used for development or testing at current or additionally agreed ranges are permitted.*

In 1975, the United States identified what seemed to be a new radar on Kamchatka Peninsula that it believed might constitute the establishment of a new Soviet ABM Test Range. When the U.S. brought this to the attention of the Soviet side, however, the U.S.S.R. indicated that a range with a radar instrumentation complex had existed on the Kamchatka Peninsula on the date of signature of the ABM Treaty. It was therefore stated by the U.S.S.R. and accepted by the U.S. that Kamchatka and Sary Shagan would be the only ABM test ranges in the U.S.S.R.

Soviet Reporting of Dismantling of Excess ABM Test Launchers

Under Article IV and Article VIII of the ABM Treaty, *each side is limited to no more than 15 ABM launchers at test ranges.*

In 1974, the U.S.S.R. notified the SCC that its excess ABM launchers had been dismantled in accordance with the agreed procedures worked out in the SCC. Because several of these launchers had been deactivated prior to entry into force of the agreed SCC procedures and not in accordance with such procedures, the U.S. raised the matter as a case of inaccurate notification or reporting. Although their reactivation would not be of strategic significance, the issue was raised by the United States so that in the future care would be taken to ensure that notification as well as dismantling or destruction was to be in strict accordance with agreed procedures.

Mobile ABM

Under Article V of the ABM Treaty, **development, testing, or deployment of a mobile ABM system or a mobile ABM radar is prohibited.**

Questions have been raised about possible Soviet development of a mobile ABM system. Since 1971, the Soviets have installed at ABM test ranges several radars associated with ABM systems currently in development. One type of radar associated with this system can be erected in a matter of months, rather than years as has been the case. Another type could be emplaced on prepared concrete foundations, which can be installed more rapidly than previous ABM systems. But they are not judged mobile in the sense of being able to move about readily or to be hidden. The U.S. recognizes that the U.S.S.R. does not have a mobile ABM system or components for such a system.

Possible Testing of an Air Defense System (SA-5) Radar in an ABM Mode

Under Article VI of the ABM Treaty, **missiles, launchers, or radars other than ABM interceptor missiles, ABM launchers, or ABM radars cannot be given capabilities to counter strategic ballistic missiles or their elements in flight trajectory.**

In 1973 and 1974, U.S. observation of Soviet tests of ballistic missiles led to the belief that a radar associated with the SA-5 surface to air missile system had been used to track strategic missiles during flight. Even though much more testing in a significantly different form would be needed before the Soviets could achieve an ABM capability for the SA-5, and extensive and observable modifications to other components of the system would have been necessary, the activity was ambiguous. The United States raised this issue, but the Soviets maintained that no Soviet air defense radar had been tested in an ABM mode. They also noted that the use of non-ABM radars for range safety or instrumentation purposes was not limited by the ABM Treaty. A short time later, the radar activity that caused concern had ceased.

After 1980
Krasnoyarsk Radar

Under Article VI of the ABM Treaty, **each Party undertakes not to deploy radars for early warning of strategic ballistic missile attack except at locations along the periphery of its national territory and oriented outward.**

Early in 1983, the Soviets began construction of a phased-array radar near Krasnoyarsk approximately 500 miles from the Soviet border, north of Mongolia and oriented northeastward. The United States contended that the Krasnoyarsk radar was similar in appearance to other Soviet early warning radars, that it was not located "along the periphery," and not oriented outward since its principal area of coverage was the Siberian land mass. The Soviets contended that the radar was for tracking satellites. Because of the location and orientation of the radar and because it did not share the technical characteristics of other radars used exclusively for tracking satellites, the United States refused to accept the Soviet interpretation. The Soviet Union stopped construction at this radar site in 1987 and has now agreed that it violates the ABM Treaty and will be dismantled.

Encoding of Missile Test Data

Under Article XV of the SALT II Treaty, **each Party is free to use various methods of transmitting telemetric information during testing including en-**

cryption except that neither Party shall engage in deliberate denial of telemetric information when such denial impedes verification of compliance with the provisions of the Treaty.

When being tested, a missile transmits radio signals to ground monitoring stations so that its performance can be assessed. These signals are also monitored by listening devices of the other side. Over the last several years, it has been reported that the Soviets have used a high level of encryption in the testing of the SS-X-20 IRBM and the SS-X-24 and SS-X-25 ICBMs. Some reports put the level as high as 60 to 100 percent encrypted during certain tests. Only when channels are blocked so as to impede ability to verify Soviet compliance could a violation be alleged. The Soviets contend this is not the case. Tentative agreement has now been reached to ban encryption.

Testing and Deployment of More Than One New ICBM

*Under Article IV of the SALT II Treaty, **each party undertakes not to flight-test or deploy new types of ICBMs, that is, types of ICBMs not flight-tested as of May 1, 1979, except that each party may flight-test and deploy one new type of light ICBM.***

The U.S. designated the MX missile as its one permitted new type. The Soviet Union has designated the SS-24, a 10-warhead ICBM, as its one permitted new type. In 1985, the U.S.S.R. apparently completed flight-testing of the SS-25, a single warhead missile with a mobile launcher. The U.S.S.R. contends that this is a permitted modernization of the SS-13, an existing single warhead ICBM. Although the SS-13 and the SS-25 both use solid fuel, the U.S. argues that the permitted increase in throw-weight has been exceeded and that the weight of its single reentry vehicle is less than the required 50 percent of the total throw-weight.

Banned Deployment of SS-16

*Under a Common Understanding in Article IV of the SALT II Treaty, **the U.S.S.R. agreed not to produce, test, or deploy ICBMs of the SS-16 type, and in particular, not to produce the SS-16 third stage, or the reentry vehicle of that missile.***

While admitting that the evidence is ambiguous and that a definite conclusion cannot be reached, the U.S. government contends that there is evidence of activities at Plesetsk that may constitute a violation of this provision of the treaty. Concerns over SS-16 deployment were expressed during the Carter administration although evidence was not deemed sufficient to raise this matter at the SCC.

Exceeding the Limits of the Threshold Test Ban Treaty (TTBT)

*Under Article I of the Threshold Test Ban Treaty, **the Parties undertake to prohibit, to prevent, and not to carry out any underground nuclear weapon test having a yield exceeding 150 kilotons at any place under its jurisdiction or control.***

In 1974, the U.S., U.S.S.R. and the United Kingdom signed the Threshold Test Ban Treaty, which prohibits testing nuclear devices underground with an explosive power (yield) of greater than 150 kilotons. They also agreed that one or two breaches would not be considered a violation. While the evidence is ambiguous and no definitive conclusions have been reached, it has been alleged that since 1978, the U.S.S.R. has conducted 14 underground tests above the 150 kiloton limit and that several were about 250 kilotons. In early 1986, a CIA report indicated that more refined evaluation of seismic data warranted a significant reduction in estimates of Soviet underground test yields.

Violation Concerns
Questions Raised by the U.S.S.R.

Prior to 1980

Shelters over Minuteman Silos

Under Article V of the Interim Agreement, *deliberate concealment measures that impede verification of compliance by national technical means are prohibited.*

Beginning in 1974, the United States used prefabricated shelters of about 2700 square feet over Minuteman silos to provide environmental protection during modernization and silo-hardening work. The Soviets classified the activity as deliberate concealment. Based on the nature of the shelters and their intended use for protection of workers, and not for concealment, the United States contended that their use was consistent with the provisions of the Interim Agreement. In 1977, the U.S. modified the use of these shelters by reducing their size by almost 50 percent.

Radar on Shemya Island

Under Article III of the ABM Treaty, *ABM systems or their components can be deployed only within one ABM deployment area centered on the Party's national capital and within one deployment area containing ICBM silo launchers.*

In 1973, the United States began construction of a new phased-array radar on Shemya Island, Alaska to be used for national technical means of verification, space tracking, and early warning. In 1975, the Soviets raised the question whether the radar was an ABM radar, which would not be permitted at this location according to the provisions of the ABM Treaty. The United States discussed this matter and eliminated any concern about possible inconsistency with the provisions of the ABM Treaty, and it became operational in early 1977.

Dismantling or Destruction of the ABM Radar under Construction at Malmstrom AFB

Under Article III and Article VIII of the ABM Treaty, *only one ABM system deployment area is permitted for defense of ICBM.*

In 1972, the United States had ABM defenses under construction in two deployment areas containing ICBM silos. Since the ABM Treaty permitted each party only one such ABM system, the United States immediately halted the construction in Malmstrom AFB, Montana according to specific procedures for dismantling or destruction. In 1974, the U.S. notified the U.S.S.R. in the SCC that Malmstrom dismantling activities had been completed. The Soviets raised a question about one detailed aspect that they felt had not been carried out in full accord with the agreement procedures. The U.S. reviewed the actions taken to dismantle the Malmstrom site and showed photographs of the before and after conditions. The question was resolved on that basis.

Atlas and Titan I Launchers

Under a protocol developed by the Standing Consultative Commission, replacement, dismantling, and destruction of strategic offensive arms must be governed by the detailed procedures of the SCC.

In 1966, the United States deactivated 177 launchers for the obsolete Atlas and Titan I ICBM systems according to SCC protocol. In 1975, the Soviets apparently perceived an ambiguity with respect to the status and conditions of these launchers based on the amount of dismantling that had been done and its effect on their possible reactivation time. The U.S. view was that these launchers were obsolete and deactivated prior to the Interim Agreement and therefore were not subject to the accompanying dismantling or destruction procedures of that agreement. However, the United States did provide some information on their condition illustrating that they could not be reactivated easily or quickly. The discussion ceased in mid-1975.

Privacy of SCC Proceedings

Under the Standing Consultative Commission Regulations-Paragraph 8, proceedings of the SCC shall be conducted in private and can be made public only with the express consent of both Commissioners.

Prior to the special SCC session held in early 1975 to discuss certain questions related to compliance, several articles appeared in various U.S. publications speculating about the possibility of certain Soviet violations of the SALT agreements purported to be from accurate intelligence information. The Soviets expressed their concern about the importance of confidentiality in the work of the SCC and were apparently particularly concerned about press items that may appear to have official U.S. government sanction. The United States discussed the usefulness of maintaining privacy of SCC negotiations and limiting speculation in the public media on SCC proceedings, but at the same time expressed the need to keep the public adequately informed.

After 1980

Deadlocked Arms Control Talks

Under Article VI of the NonProliferation Treaty, the Parties undertake to pursue negotiations in good faith on effective measures relating to cessation of the nuclear arms race at an early date and to nuclear disarmament, and on a treaty on general and complete disarmament under strict and effective international control.

The U.S.S.R. charges the U.S. with violating the obligation to conduct arms control talks in "a spirit of good will." It blames the U.S. for the arms control stalemate, for failing to ratify the SALT II Treaty, and for unilaterally discontinuing talks on the general and complete prohibition of nuclear weapon tests, on Indian Ocean naval force restraints, and on antisatellite systems.

Deployment of Missiles in Europe

Under Article XII and XIII of the SALT II Treaty, each Party undertakes not to circumvent the provisions of the Treaty through any other state or states or in any other manner, and not to assume any international obligations that would conflict with this Treaty.

The U.S.S.R. claims that the U.S. deployment in western Europe of nuclear arms—the Pershing II ballistic missiles and long-range cruise missiles capable of reaching targets in the U.S.S.R.—are additions to the U.S. strategic offensive arsenal and therefore a violation of these provisions of the SALT II Treaty. In the light of this deployment, the Soviet Union questions the credibility of the U.S. statement that "it would refrain from any actions undermining existing agreements on strategic arms," even though the Treaty had not been ratified.

Shelters over Minuteman Silos

Under Article V of the Interim Agreement, **deliberate concealment measures that impede verification of compliance by national technical means is prohibited.**

The Soviet Union states that it has repeatedly raised the question of shelters over the Minuteman II and Titan II missile launchers. They classify this activity as deliberate concealment of work to refit launchers of the Minuteman II, and claim that once refitted, these launchers do not differ in practical terms from the launchers of Minuteman III missiles. They further conjecture that MIRVed Minuteman III missiles are being deployed in these silos which would also constitute a violation of the SALT II Treaty limiting the number of MIRVed ICBMs. The question of these shelters had been previously raised and considered resolved by the reduction in their size.

Privacy of SCC Proceedings

Under the Standing Consultative Commission Regulations, Paragraph 8, **proceedings of the SCC shall be conducted in private and can be made public only with the express consent of both Commissioners.**

The U.S.S.R. continues to express concern about alleged U.S. violation of the confidentiality of SCC discussions. The U.S.S.R. insists that this must be stopped.

Abiding by the Protocol of the SALT II Treaty

Under the Protocol to the SALT II Treaty, **the deployment of weapons about which both sides had the greatest difficulty in agreeing–ground-launched and sea-launched cruise missiles and mobile ICBMs–is prohibited.**

The Soviets contend that there has been accelerated development of new strategic offensive forces such as the MX, Midgetman, nuclear-powered submarines armed with Trident missiles, B-1B and Stealth strategic bombers, multi-purpose shuttle space systems, and long-range air, sea, and land-based cruise missiles. They claim that this is in violation of the Protocol to the SALT II Treaty and contradicts the recognized principles of international law as well as fundamental Soviet-American accords—which clearly stipulate that neither side shall strive for military superiority and shall be guided by the principal of equal security.

Exceeding the Limits of the Threshold Test Ban Treaty

Under Article I of the Threshold Test Ban Treaty, **the Parties undertake to prohibit, to prevent, and not to carry out any underground nuclear weapon test having a yield exceeding 150 kilotons at any place under its jurisdiction or control.**

According to data gathered by the U.S.S.R., the United States is charged with violating the Treaty by continuing to test nuclear devices underground over the yield of 150 kilotons.

Radioactive Debris

*Under Article I of the Limited Test Ban Treaty of 1963, **the Parties are prohibited from testing nuclear weapons in the atmosphere, outer space, or under water, or any other environment if the explosion causes radio-active debris to be present outside the territorial limits of the State under whose jurisdiction or control such explosion is conducted.***

The U.S.S.R. says it has approached the U.S. about the ejection of radioactive substances beyond the national territorial limits of the U.S. as a result of underground nuclear explosions. They also claim that the U.S. has refused to conduct talks on the conclusion of an agreement on general and complete prohibition of nuclear weapon tests as well as rejecting the Soviet proposed moratorium on all nuclear weapon tests.

Radar Shemya Island and PAVE PAW Radars

*Under Article III and Article VI of the ABM Treaty, **ABM systems or their components can be deployed only within one ABM deployment area centered on the Party's national capital and within one deployment area containing ICBM silo launchers; each Party undertakes not to give missiles, launchers, or radars, other than ABM interceptor missiles, ABM launchers, or ABM radars, capabilities to counter strategic ballistic missiles or their elements in flight trajectory, and not to test them in an ABM mode.***

In 1973, the question of a radar station on Shemya Island was raised by the Soviets, and the U.S. interpretation that its use was for verification, space-tracking, and early warning purposes was accepted. The U.S.S.R. now claims that this radar station has radar system elements that can be utilized for ABM purposes; that shelters were used over anti-missile launcher silos; that work is being conducted to create mobile ABM radar systems and space-based ABM systems; that the Minuteman I ICBMs are being tested for anti-missile capabilities; and that multiple warheads are being developed for anti-missiles—all in contradiction to the provisions of this Treaty. The U.S.S.R. also charges that the new PAVE PAW radar stations being deployed on the Atlantic and Pacific coasts and in the South provide radar-backing for an ABM defense and therefore is in violation of this Treaty. The Kremlin states that no measures have yet been taken to allay the U.S.S.R. concern. Also of asserted concern to the U.S.S.R. is President Reagan's endorsement in March 1983 of space-based ABM systems that would clearly mean abrogation of the Treaty.

Source of Information: "The President's Report to the Congress on Soviet Noncompliance with Arms Control Agreements," *The White House, Office of the Press Secretary*

"Background Paper on Compliance Issues," *The Arms Control Association*

"Arms Control and Disarmament Agreements," U.S. Arms Control and *Disarmament Agency*

Section V

- **The Effects of Nuclear War**

    Blast
    Direct Nuclear Radiation
    Thermal Radiation
    Fires
    Electromagnetic Pulse
    Fallout
    The TTAPS Report—A Nuclear Winter

- **Arms Control Terms**

- **Acronyms**

"A nuclear holocaust would destroy the living and cancel the unborn in the same blow."

Jonathan Schell

The Effects of Nuclear War

The energy of a nuclear explosion is released in a number of different ways:

- an **explosive blast** that is qualitatively similar to the blast from ordinary chemical explosions but has more devastating effects because it is typically so much larger;
- direct **nuclear radiation**;
- direct **thermal radiation**, most of which takes the form of visible light;
- pulses of electrical and magnetic energy called **electromagnetic pulse** (EMP);
- the creation of a variety of radioactive particles that are thrown up into the air by the force of the blast and are called **radioactive fallout** when they return to earth.

The distribution of the nuclear bomb's energy among these effects depends on its size and on the details of its design, but a general description is possible.

Blast

Most immediate damage to cities from large weapons comes from the explosive blast. The blast drives air away from the site of the explosion producing sudden changes in air pressure called "static overpressure" that can crush objects and destroy buildings. It also produces high winds called "dynamic pressure" that destroy people and objects such as trees and utility poles.

For the most part, blast kills people by indirect means. Most blast deaths result from the collapse of occupied buildings, from people being blown from buildings and into objects, or people being struck by flying objects.

Direct Nuclear Radiation

Nuclear weapons inflict ionizing radiation on people, animals, and plants in two different ways. *Direct radiation* occurs at the time of the explosion; it can be very intense, but its range is limited. *Fallout radiation* is received from particles that are made radioactive by the effects of the explosion and subsequently distributed at varying distances from the site of the blast.

For large nuclear weapons, the range of intense *direct radiation* is less than the range of *lethal blast* and *thermal radiation* effects. However, in the case of smaller weapons, "direct radiation" may be the lethal effect with the greatest range. Direct radiation did substantial damage to the residents of Hiroshima and Nagasaki.

Thermal Radiation

Approximately 35 percent of the energy from a nuclear explosion is an intense burst of *thermal radiation*, i.e., heat. The effects are roughly comparable to the effect of a 2-second flash from an enormous sunlamp. Since thermal radiation travels at the speed of light, the flash of light and heat precedes the blast wave by several seconds—just as lightning is seen before the thunder is heard.

The visible light will produce "flashblindness" in people who are looking in the direction of the explosion. This flashblindness would last for several minutes, after which recovery would be total. A one-megaton explosion could cause flashblindness at distances as great as 13 miles on a clear day or 53 miles on a clear night.

Skin burns result from higher intensities of light and therefore take place closer to the point of explosion. A one-megaton explosion can cause

First degree burns at distances of about 7 miles;

Second degree burns at distances of about 6 miles, producing blisters that lead to infection if untreated and permanent scars; and

Third degree burns at distances of up to 5 miles, destroying skin tissue.

If 24 to 30 percent of the body is covered with second or third degree burns, this will result in serious shock and probably prove fatal unless prompt, specialized medical care is available. The entire

United States has facilities to treat 1000 to 2000 severe burn cases—a single nuclear weapon could produce more than 10,000.

Fires

The **thermal radiation** from a nuclear explosion can directly ignite kindling materials. Fires most likely to spread are those caused by thermal radiation passing through windows, igniting beds and overstuffed furniture inside houses.

Another possible source of fires, which might be more damaging in urban areas, is indirect. **Blast damage** to stoves, water heaters, furnaces, electrical circuits, or gas lines would ignite fires where fuel is plentiful.

It is possible that individual fires, whether caused by "thermal radiation" or by "blast damage" to utilities, furnaces, and so on would coalesce into a mass fire that would consume all structures over a large area. Mass fires could be of two kinds:

- a **firestorm** in which violent inrushing winds create extremely high temperatures but prevent the fire from spreading radially outwards such as the firestorms experienced in Hamburg, Tokyo, and Hiroshima in World War II; and
- a **conflagration** in which a fire spreads along a front such as the Great Chicago fire and the San Francisco earthquake fire.

Electromagnetic Pulse (EMP)

Electromagnetic pulse is an **electromagnetic wave** similar to radio waves that results from secondary reactions occurring when the nuclear gamma radiation is absorbed in the air or ground. Most equipment designed to protect electrical facilities from lightning works too slowly to be effective against EMP.

There is no evidence that EMP is a physical threat to humans. However electrical or electronic systems, particularly those connected to long wires such as powerlines or antennas, can undergo physical damage such as a shorting of a capacitor or burnout of a transistor, and at a lesser level, a temporary operational upset.

Fallout

While any nuclear explosion in the atmosphere produces some fallout, the **fallout** is far greater if the burst is on the surface or at least low enough for the fireball to touch the ground. Fallout from air bursts alone poses long-term health hazards, but they are trivial compared to the other consequences of a nuclear attack. The significant hazards come from particles scooped up from the ground and irradiated by the nuclear explosion.

The radioactive particles in the stem of the familiar mushroom cloud, that rise only a short distance, will fall back to earth within a matter of minutes, landing close to the center of the explosion. Such particles are unlikely to be the cause of many deaths because they will fall in areas where most people have already been killed. The radioactivity, however, will complicate efforts at rescue or eventual reconstruction.

The radioactive particles that rise higher will be carried some distance by the wind before returning to earth. Hence the area and intensity of the fallout are strongly influenced by local weather conditions. Much of the material is simply blown downwind in a long plume. "Wind direction" can make an enormous difference. "Rainfall" can also have a significant influence on the ways in which radiation from smaller weapons is deposited, since rain will carry contaminated particles to the ground. The areas receiving such contaminated rainfall would become **hot spots** with greater radiation intensity than their surroundings. When the radiation intensity from fallout is great enough to pose an immediate threat to health, fallout will generally be visible as a thin layer of dust.

Some radioactive particles will be thrust into the stratosphere and may not return to earth for some years. In this case only particularly long-lived particles pose a threat, and they would be dispersed around the world over a range of latitudes. Some fallout from U.S. and Soviet weapons tests in the 1950s and early 1960s can still be detected.

The biological effects of fallout radiation are substantially the same as those from direct radiation. People exposed to enough fallout radiation will die, and those exposed to lesser amounts may become ill.

The TTAPS Report—A Nuclear Winter

In late 1983, a group of 40 distinguished scientists released a study, the TTAPS Report, on the global atmospheric and climatic effects that would be caused by a nuclear war.

Summarized, the four known principal consequences that would occur after a nuclear war are: obscuring smoke in the troposphere (7 to 10 miles from the earth's surface); obscuring dust in the stratosphere (upper portion of the atmosphere); fallout of radioactive debris; and partial destruction of the ozone layer, which shields and protects the earth from the deadly ultraviolet radiation of the sun.

Based on new findings concerning the earth's thin ozone layer, the report concludes that the dust, especially the soot, would absorb ordinary visible light from the sun, thus reducing the amount of sunlight penetrating the earth's surface. The heavy toxic overcast would last for months and longer, making photosynthesis and thereby all plant growth impossible. Land temperatures would drop to 13 degrees below zero. Carl Sagan, the renowned scientist, predicts a **nuclear winter** where temperatures would drop so catastrophically that virtually all crops and farm animals would be destroyed as would most varieties of uncultivated or undomesticated food supplies. Most survivors of heat, blast, and radiation thus would starve.

This study has been endorsed by over 100 scientists and biologists including scientists from the Soviet Union. A Department of Defense study in 1985 acknowledged that its premises had scientific validity and could not be cursorily dismissed.

Source of Information: "The Effects of Nuclear War," 79-60080
Office of Technology Assessment

"The Effects of Nuclear War,"
U.S. Arms Control and Disarmament Agency; Office of Operations Analysis

"Nuclear Winter: Global Consequences of Multiple Nuclear Explosions,"
The TTAPS Report; The Center on the Consequences of Nuclear War

Arms Control Terms

air-launched cruise missile—*See* cruise missile.

airborne warning and control system (AWACS)—A flying command post. AWACS has the capacity to identify hostile aircraft and to control friendly air forces in either offensive or defensive missions.

anti-ballistic missile (ABM) system—A system of missiles and radars capable of defending against a ballistic-missile attack by destroying incoming offensive missiles. The defensive missiles may be armed with either nuclear or non-nuclear warheads.

anti-submarine warfare (ASW)—The detection, identification, tracking, and destruction of hostile submarines. ASW can be either strategic (aimed at neutralizing an opponent's ballistic-missile submarines), or tactical (concerned with the pursuit and destruction of submarines in a local situation for missions such as convoy defense and aircraft carrier defense).

arms control—Any unilateral action or multilateral plan, arrangement, or process, resting upon explicit or implicit international agreement, which limits or regulates any aspect of the following: the production, numbers, type configuration, and performance characteristics of weapon systems (including related command and control, logistics support, and intelligence arrangements or mechanisms); and the numerical strength, organization, equipment, deployment, or employment of the armed forces retained by the parties.

arms limitation—*See* arms control.

arms transfer—The sale or grant of arms from one nation to another.

ballistic missile—A missile, classified by range, that moves on a free-falling trajectory under the influence of gravity.

ballistic missile defense (BMD)—*See* ABM system.

binary nerve gas—A toxic gas created by the mixture of two relatively harmless chemicals during the final trajectory stage of a missile, bomb, or shell in which the gases are loaded. Because its two components are non-toxic until they are combined, binary gas can be stored and handled more easily than other toxic gases.

bomber—An aircraft, usually classified by range, capable of delivering nuclear and non-nuclear ordnance. Long-range bombers are those capable of traveling 6000 or more miles on one load of fuel; medium-range bombers can travel between 3500 and 6000 miles without refueling.

breeder reactor—A reactor that produces more nuclear fuel than it consumes while generating power.

circular error probable (CEP)—A measure of missile accuracy. It is the radius of a circle around a target in which 50 percent of the missiles aimed at that target will land.

civil defense—All those activities and measures designed to minimize the effects upon the civilian population caused by an enemy attack upon the United States; to deal with immediate emergency conditions and to effectuate emergency restoration of vital utilities and facilities destroyed by such attack.

command, control, communication, and intelligence (C³I)—The "nerves" of military operations, that is, information-processing systems used to detect, assess, and respond to actual and potential military and political crisis situations or conflicts. C³I includes systems that manage materiel and manpower during crises or conflicts, as well as in peacetime.

confidence-building measures—Measures taken to demonstrate a nation's lack of belligerent or hostile *intent*, as distinguished from measures that actually reduce military *capabilities*. Confidence-building measures can be negotiated or unilateral. The division between confidence-building measures and arms control measures is not strict; the former may involve, for example, troop withdrawals, while the latter may aim more at securing trust than limiting weaponry.

counterforce—Directed against an opponent's military forces and military industry. Used to describe military strategies, attacks, weapons, and so on.

countervalue—Directed against an opponent's civilian and economic centers. Used to describe military strategies, attacks, weapons, and so on.

crisis stability—A strategic situation in which neither side has an incentive to use nuclear weapons during a crisis.

cruise missile—A pilotless missile, propelled by an air-breathing jet engine, that flies in the atmosphere. Cruise missiles may be armed with either conventional or nuclear warheads and launched from an aircraft, a submarine or surface ship, or land-based platform.

damage limitation—The capacity to reduce damage from a nuclear attack by passive or active defenses or by striking the opponent's forces in a counterforce attack.

dense pack—A basing proposal for the MX missile in which silos are placed very close together. Supporters of the dense pack system argue that incoming missile "fratricide" will increase MX survivability.

deterrence—Dissuasion of a potential adversary from initiating an attack or conflict, often by the threat of unacceptable retaliatory damage. Nuclear deterrence is usually contrasted with the concept of nuclear defense, the strategy and forces for limiting damage, if deterrence fails. Some hold that a strategy of nuclear defense may also have a deterrent effect, if it can reduce the destructive potential of a nuclear attack.

disarmament—In UN usage, all measures related to the prevention, limitation, reduction, or elimination of weapons and military forces. See general and complete disarmament.

fallout—The spread of radioactive particles from clouds of debris produced by nuclear blasts. "Local fallout" falls to the Earth's surface within twenty-four hours of the blast.

first strike—An initial attack with nuclear weapons. A *disarming* first strike is one in which the attacker attempts to destroy all or a large portion of its adversary's strategic nuclear forces before they can be launched. A *preemptive* first strike is one in which a nation launches its attack first on the presumption that the adversary is about to attack.

first use—The introduction of nuclear weapons into a strategic tactical conflict. See first strike. A no-first-use pledge by a nation obliges it not to be the first to introduce nuclear weapons in a conflict.

fission—The process of splitting atomic nuclei through bombardment of neutrons. This process yields vast quantities of energy as well as more neutrons capable of initiating further fission.

fractionation—The division of bomber or missile payload into separate re-entry vehicles.

fratricide—The destruction or degradation of the accuracy and effectiveness of an attacking nuclear weapon by the nearby explosion of another attacking nuclear weapon.

freeze—See nuclear freeze.

fusion—The process of combining atomic nuclei to form a single heavier element or nucleus and to release large amounts of energy.

general and complete disarmament (GCD)—The total abandonment of military forces and weapons (other than internal police forces) by all nations at the same time, usually foreseen as occurring through an agreed schedule of force reductions. In 1961, in the so-called McCloy-Zorin Principles, the United States and the U.S.S.R. agreed that their negotiations would have GCD as their ultimate objective.

ground-launched cruise missile (GLCM)—See cruise missile.

hard or hardened target—A target protected against the blast, heat, and radiation effects of nuclear weapons of specific yields. Hardening is usually accomplished by means of earth and reinforced concrete and is measured by the number of pounds per square inch of blast overpressure which a target can withstand.

intercontinental ballistic missile (ICBM)—A ballistic missile with a range of 4000 or more nautical miles. Conventionally, the term ICBM is used only for land-based systems to differentiate them from submarine-launched ballistic missiles, which also have an intercontinental range.

intermediate nuclear forces (INF)—A term coined by U.S. officials to emphasize the links between U.S. strategic weapons and theater weapons in Europe. In its original meaning, it was synonymous with long-range theater nuclear forces (LRTNF). More recently, it has been expanded to include all TNF except battlefield weapons. Negotiations between the U.S. and the U.S.S.R., opened in November 1981, seek to limit the European-based, intermediate-range nuclear forces of both sides. *See also* theater nuclear forces, long-range theater nuclear forces.

kiloton—A measure of the yield of a nuclear weapon equivalent to 1000 tons of TNT.

launch-on-warning doctrine—A strategic doctrine under which a nation's bombers and land-based missiles would be launched on receipt of warning (from satellites and other early-warning systems) that an opponent had launched its missiles. This doctrine is sometimes also called "launch on positive (or confirmed) notification of attack" to distinguish between possible and actual attack. Sometimes recommended for use when there is uncertainty over the ability of fixed-site strategic weapons (e.g., ICBMs) to survive an attack, a launch-on-warning doctrine is viewed as destabilizing in a crisis situation.

light-water reactor—The most common type of nuclear power reactor. It is fueled by enriched uranium. The spent fuel of a light-water reactor contains significant amounts of plutonium that could be used to make nuclear explosives.

Mark 12A warhead—A new warhead for the Minuteman III missile. The increased accuracy and yield of the Mark 12A re-entry vehicles in the warhead will increase the ability of the Minuteman III missiles to destroy hardened Soviet missile silos and other targets.

megaton—A measure of the yield of a nuclear weapon equivalent to 1,000,000 tons of TNT.

missile experimental (MX)—A U.S. ICBM originally intended to replace the (older) ICBM force during the 1980s. This more accurate, powerful, and destructive missile could be deployed in either a single silo or mobile mode and would be capable of destroying Soviet missile silos. The MX force has been limited to 50 and the question of rail-mobile basing remains unresolved.

multiple independently-targetable re-entry vehicle (MIRV)—A package of two or more re-entry vehicles that can be carried by a single ballistic missile and delivered on separate targets. The term MIRV is also commonly used for a missile with a MIRVed warhead or for the process of switching from single to multiple re-entry vehicles.

mutual assured destruction—A concept of reciprocal deterrence that rests on the ability of the two nuclear superpowers to inflict unacceptable damage on one another after surviving a nuclear first strike.

national technical means (NTM)—A method of verifying compliance with negotiated arms control agreements generally consistent with the recognized provisions of international law, commonly understood as surveillance by satellite and aerial reconnaissance.

neutron bomb—A tactical nuclear warhead designed to enhance radiation effects. It would be carried on artillery shells and short-range missiles, primarily for defense against a tank and heavy armored attack by the Warsaw Pact. The purported advantage is minimization of blast damage in friendly territory.

no-first-use doctrine—A no-first-use pledge by a nation obliges it not to introduce nuclear weapons first into a conflict. *See* first use.

nuclear freeze—The generic term for a variety of proposals calling for a halt to the testing, production, and deployment of all nuclear weapons and delivery systems. Proposals have been introduced in both houses of Congress, numerous local and town councils, and a variety of state legislatures.

nuclear fuel cycle—Any process for developing, utilizing, and disposing of nuclear fuels.

nuclear weapon-free zone—An area in which the production and deployment of nuclear weapons is prohibited.

on-site inspection—A method of verifying compliance with an arms control agreement whereby representatives of an international or other designated organization, or of the parties to the agreement, are given direct access to view force deployments or weapon systems.

parity—A level of forces in which opposing nations possess approximately equal capabilities.

peaceful nuclear explosion (PNE)—The non-military use of nuclear detonations for such purposes as stimulating natural gas, recovering oil shale, diverting rivers, or excavating.

Pershing II—Deployment began in 1983, and the INF Treaty of 1988 requires its elimination.

plutonium—An element not found in nature that is created as a waste product of nuclear reactors. Plutonium can be used to make nuclear weapons.

pounds per square inch (psi)—A measure of nuclear blast overpressure or dynamic pressure used to calculate the effects of a nuclear detonation or the ability of a structure to withstand a nuclear blast.

preemptive strike—A damage-limiting attack launched in anticipation of an opponent's attack.

proliferation—The spread of weapons, usually nuclear weapons. Horizontal proliferation refers to the acquisition of nuclear weapons by states not previously possessing them. Vertical proliferation refers to increases in the nuclear arsenals of those states already possessing nuclear weapons.

re-entry vehicle—That part of a ballistic missile designed to re-enter the earth's atmosphere in the terminal portion of its trajectory.

reprocessing plant—A facility required to separate the uranium and plutonium present in spent reactor fuel. The plutonium recovered through reprocessing can be reused as reactor fuel or for nuclear explosives.

sea-launched cruise missile (SLCM)—See cruise missile.

second strike—A follow-up or rataliatory attack after an opponent's first strike. Second-strike capability describes the capacity to attack after suffering a first strike. The U.S. strategy of deterrence is premised on high confidence in the ability of the United States to deliver a nuclear second strike that would inflict unacceptable damage on the nation that struck first.

Standing Consultative Commission (SCC)—A joint U.S.-U.S.S.R. negotiating body, established by the ABM Treaty, that meets semi-annually to review implementation of the ABM Treaty and other strategic arms limitation agreements in force.

strategic—Relating to a nation's offensive or defensive military potential including its geographical location and its resources, and economic, political, and military strength. The term *strategic* is used to denote those weapons or forces capable of directly affecting another nation's war-fighting ability, as distinguished from tactical or theater weapons or forces.

Strategic Arms Limitation Talks (SALT)—Negotiations between the United States and the U.S.S.R. initiated in 1969 that seek to limit the strategic nuclear forces, both offensive and defensive, of both sides.

Strategic Arms Reduction Talks (START)—Negotiations between the U.S. and U.S.S.R., formerly named SALT, which were started in June 1982 to seek reductions in the strategic arsenals of both sides. The change in name came as a result of the Reagan administration's desire to emphasize reductions rather than mere limitations in nuclear weapons.

Strategic Defense Initiative (SDI)—An anti-ballistic missile program intended to intercept Soviet missiles during all three phases of Soviet missile flight—the boost phase, the mid-course phase, and the terminal phase.

Strategic Talks on Prevention of Nuclear War (STOP)—An arms control negotiating position that focuses specifically on measures to achieve stability and prevent the use of nuclear weapons.

submarine-launched ballistic missile (SLBM)—Any ballistic missile launched from a submarine.

tactical—Relating to battlefield operations as distinguished from theater or strategic operations. Tactical weapons or forces are those designed for combat with opposing military forces rather than for reaching the rear areas of the opponent or the opponent's homeland, and require theater or strategic weapons, respectively.

telemetry—The transmission of electronic signals by missiles to earth. Monitoring these signals aids in evaluating a weapon's performance and provides a way of verifying weapon tests undertaken by an adversary.

theater nuclear weapon (TNW)—A nuclear weapon, usually of longer range and larger yield than a tactical nuclear weapon, which can be used in theater operations. Many strategic nuclear weapons can be used in theater operations, but not all theater nuclear weapons are designed for strategic use. The Soviet SS-20 mobile missile is generally considered a theater nuclear weapon, as are the nuclear-capable U.S. fighter/bombers deployed in the Far East and Europe and the U.S. Lance missile.

throw-weight—The maximum weight of the warheads, guidance unit, and penetration aids that can be delivered by a missile over a particular range and in a stated trajectory.

triad—U.S. strategic forces that are composed of three parts: land-based intercontinental ballistic missiles; submarine-launched ballistic missiles; and long-range bombers.

uranium—A heavy silvery-white metallic element, radioactive, easily oxidized, and having 14 known isotopes of which U238 is the most abundant in nature.

verticle short take-off and landing (V/STOL)—Relating to the ability of an aircraft to clear vertically a 50-foot obstacle within 1500 feet after takeoff or stop within 1500 feet over a 50-foot obstacle in landing. An advantage of V/STOL aircraft is that they are able to operate nearer the forward edge of the battle area.

warhead—That part of a missile, torpedo, rocket, or other munition that contains either the nuclear or thermonuclear system, chemical or biological agent, or inert materials intended to inflict damage.

yield—The force of a nuclear explosion expressed as the equivalent of the energy produced by tons of TNT. *See* kiloton and megaton.

Source of Information: "SALT II Agreement," Selected Documents No. 12A
U.S. Department of State

"A Glossary of Arms Control Terms,"
The Arms Control Association

Acronyms Used in the Nuclear Weapons Issue

ABM	Anti-Ballistic Missile
ALBM	Air-Launched Ballistic Missile
ALCM	Air-Launched Cruise Missile
ASBM	Air-to-Surface Ballistic Missile
ASW	Anti-Submarine Warfare
AWACS	Airborne Warning and Control System
BMD	Ballistic Missile Defense
CCD	Conference of the Committee on Disarmament
CD	Committee on Disarmament
CEP	Circular Error Probable
CFE	Conventional Forces in Europe
C³I	Command, Control, Communications, and Intelligence
CM	Cruise Missile
CSCE	Conference on Security and Cooperation in Europe
CTBT	Comprehensive Test Ban Treaty
DOD	Department of Defense
FBS	Forward-Based System
GLCM	Ground-Launched Cruise Missile
HB	Heavy Bomber
ICBM	InterContinental Ballistic Missile
INF	Intermediate Nuclear Forces
IRBM	Intermediate-Range Ballistic Missile
KT	Kiloton—1000 Tons of TNT
LRTNF	Long-Range Theater Nuclear Force
MBFR	Mutual and Balanced Forces Reductions Talks
MIRV	Multiple Independently-Targetable Re-entry Vehicle
MRBM	Medium-Range Ballistic Missile
MT	Megaton—1,000,000 Tons of TNT
MX	Missile eXperimental
NPT	NonProliferation Treaty
NTM	National Technical Means
PSI	Pounds Per Square Inch
R&D	Research and Development
RV	Reentry Vehicle
SALT	Strategic Arms Limitation Talks
SAM	Surface-to-Air Missile
SCC	Standing Consultative Commission
SDI	Strategic Defense Initiative (Star Wars)
SLBM	Submarine-Launched Ballistic Missile
SLCM	Sea-Launched Cruise Missile
SRAM	Short-Range Attack Missile
SRBM	Short-Range Ballistic Missile
SSBN	Nuclear-Propelled Ballistic-Missile-Bearing Submarine
START	Strategic Arms Reduction Talks

STOP	Strategic Talks on Prevention of Nuclear War
TTBT	Threshold Test Ban Treaty

Source of Information: The majority of acronyms compiled from:
"A Glossary of Arms Control Terms,"
The Arms Control Association

Index